Happy

FATHERS

DAy

SweetHeart

I Love you -

A Question of
HONOR

A Question of
HONOR

*The Cheating Scandal That Rocked
Annapolis and a Midshipman Who
Decided to Tell the Truth*

★ ★ ★

Jeffrey Gantar & Tom Patten
with Michael O'Donnell

ZondervanPublishingHouse
Grand Rapids, Michigan

A Division of HarperCollins*Publishers*

A Question of Honor
Copyright © 1996 by Jeffrey Gantar, Michael O'Donnell, and Tom Patten

Requests for information should be addressed to:

ZondervanPublishingHouse
Grand Rapids, Michigan 49530

Library of Congress Cataloging-in-Publication Data

Gantar, Jeffrey, 1972–
    A question of honor : the cheating scandal that rocked Annapolis and a midshipman
who decided to tell the truth / Jeffrey Gantar and Tom Patten with Michael O'Donnell.
    p. cm.
    ISBN 0-310-20912-9 (hardcover)
    1. Gantar, Jeffrey, 1972– . 2. United States Naval Academy—History.   3. College
student government—Maryland—Annapolis.   4. Cheating (Education)—Maryland—
Annapolis. I. Patten, Tom, 1948– . II. O'Donnell, Michael, 1956– . III. Title.
V415.P1G36   1996
359'.0071'173—dc20   96-12533
                                                          CIP

This edition printed on acid-free paper and meets the American National Standards Institute
Z39.48 standard.

All Scripture quotations, unless otherwise indicated, are taken from the *Holy Bible: New
International Version®*. NIV®. Copyright © 1973, 1978, 1984 by International Bible Society.
Used by permission of ZondervanPublishingHouse. All rights reserved.

Edited by John Sloan and Mary McNeil
Interior design by Sherri L. Hoffman

Published in association with the literary agency of Alive Communications, Inc., 1465 Kelly
Johnson Boulevard #320, Colorado Springs, CO 80920

Printed in the United States of America

---

96 97 98 99 00 01 02 /❖ DH/ 10 9 8 7 6 5 4 3 2 1

To our wives: Angie, Karen, and Rachel
and
To our parents: Mark and Julie; Roy and Gerry;
and Bill and Valia
and
To our siblings: Mark and Dorie; Dana and Berne; Billy,
Dee, and Richard

CONTENTS

ACKNOWLEDGMENTS

To Thom Lemmons, novelist, editor, and publisher *par excellence,* we'd like to say thank-you for your invaluable assistance and inexhaustible creativity in manuscript development, which has made *A Question of Honor* possible. We'd also like to thank our agent, Greg Johnson, for seeing the possibilities and finding us just the right publisher. To our editor, John Sloan, and to the whole publishing team at Zondervan—we appreciate your desire to present lessons of faith and integrity. And thanks to Morley Safer and *60 Minutes* for their genuine attempt to present the truth.

Jeffrey Gantar: Thanks to my coauthor, Tom "Doc" Patten, for helping me to experience the healing power of truth; my writer, Dr. Michael O'Donnell, for writing with compelling intensity and narrative power; Grandpa Karl Engdahl and Grandma Berta Engdahl, for your love and guidance; Grandpa Mark Gantar, Louise, and Grandma Margo, for being the best grandparents I could ask for and for Grandpa Mark's honorable service in the U.S. Navy, which has been a shining example to me; my high school calculus teacher, Gerry Manfred, and my high school baseball coach, Don Ressa, for helping me to excel and to receive an appointment to the Academy; my best friend while growing up, Mark Sodorff, for spending hours practicing baseball with me; my confirmation teacher, Pastor Norm Olson, for your help in my spiritual growth, my Academy classmates,

Michael Carter, Rich Rivera, John Greene, John Formoso, for their camaraderie that helped me make it to my senior year; my close friends at the Academy, Brian Pirko, Dusty Rhodes, Rob Doherty, Casey Williams, and Chris Fassari, for letting me lean on you during the tough times; the "Lunch Club"—Jim, Billy, Arnold, Shenan, Charlie, Peter, Tom, and Andy, for helping me to deal with my separation from the Academy; my Academy chaplain, Father Hines, for not giving up on me and showing me the correct path to walk.

Tom Patten: I would especially like to thank Captains McCullough and Brunza and Dr. Austin, who have been my mentors in all the best senses of that word. I appreciate Dennis Webber in many ways; it was he who got the ball rolling on the way to this book. I owe a great debt to our writer, Dr. Michael O'Donnell, for being the path to the realization of a dream and for being one of that rare species—a true friend. To Jeff Gantar: my deep appreciation for him as the source of many gifts, challenges, and inspirations. I would like to acknowledge two groups, the "Lunch Club" (Andy, Arnold, Billy, Charlie, Jeff, Jim, Peter, and Shenan) and "GGG" (Alan, Brian, Cherisse, Dana, Israel, Julie, Marsha, and Sarah). I am especially grateful to the outstanding faculty of the psychology department at Abilene Christian University for giving me a place; to my graduate assistants Cherisse and Duncan, who got me through the first year; and to Scott, Jennifer, and Amy, who have filled some very big shoes. My clients and students have always challenged and taught me, and I am deeply appreciative of them. To my second families, especially Bob, Dixie, Ginny, and Guy, thanks for making me a part of your lives. And, making the first last, to my kids, Todd, Shauna, and Amber, who are the light and pride of my life, I love you always.

I'M SITTING IN MY apartment in Seattle, waiting ... Waiting for the commercial break to be over and for *60 Minutes* to resume. When it does, I'll be watching myself on the television screen, telling Morley Safer, God, and several million of my closest friends about how a nice, all-American boy like me got tangled up in the worst cheating scandal in the 150-year history of the United States Naval Academy.

As I wait, I'm thinking back to when the interview was taped, four months ago in April, 1994. I remember walking into the presidential suite of the Loew's Annapolis hotel, amid a serpentine tangle of cables and electrical cords. Technicians were scurrying about, setting lights, checking sound levels.

The producer, a thirty-something woman with dark brown hair and a no-nonsense attitude had been prompting me about what to expect when the tape started rolling. "Jeff, try to think of your interview as a conversation with a friend. Mr. Safer will ask you what he thinks our viewers most want to know. Be sure to look at him, not at the camera. Keep your answers as short and to the point as possible."

To the point. But what was the point, and why was I there? What did I most want the folks in Televisionland to know about this time in my life, when all the wheels were coming off?

How could I make them understand what these days meant? How could I show them what it was like to watch my dreams being dismembered?

And—who would care? After all, this interview wasn't about the Jeff Gantar story, it was about the Naval Academy cheating story. I was there primarily to satisfy America's curiosity about what a cheater looked like, about what a cheater thought about, and how he justified himself—and, above all, why he would freely admit to doing such a thing. Who would care in the least about the human beings who had been crushed in the process? Who would really care about the personal history that had brought me to that moment of shame—and beyond? Who would care that, even in that dark tunnel of failure and dashed hopes, I had found my own private salvation, found something more important than a diploma from the Academy and a commission in the United States Navy?

Angie sits down beside me on the couch. I glance at her, and she tries to smile at me. She knows what watching this interview is doing to me, but she also knows I can't help watching. I'm reliving it all again, remembering the abandonment and helplessness I felt when my world crashed. I grab her hand and hold on to it like a lifeline.

The show comes on. They're showing clips of the Graduation Parade, of the Class of 1994 throwing their covers in the air. Then they cut to still shots of me and several of my classmates. "All of these midshipmen expected to be there," the voice-over says, " . . . and none of them were."

May 25, 1994 should have been the most victorious day of my life. Instead, it's a day I desperately wish I could forget—but I can't . . .

On Graduation Day, I was about thirty miles away from the Yard, in Baltimore, at Angie's apartment. Looking back on it, the experience seems almost surreal, like a Salvador Dalí landscape. I was enraged, confused, angry—and dazed, apathetic, listless, limp. Thirty miles away, my classmates were celebrating the most victorious day of their lives, a celebration I had savored during my four long, grinding years at the Naval Academy. But here I was in Angie's apartment with absolutely nothing to do except stare into the empty hole in my world and ask myself—what happened? When I replay them in my mind, the images of those days are half-remembered, haphazard bits and pieces I still can't quite put together.

I wandered aimlessly through the apartment, trying vainly not to think about the only thing I could possibly think about. In my mind's eye, I could see what was happening at the stadium. For three years I'd lived through Commissioning Week, the dizzy, headlong final week of the term that culminated in the graduation and commissioning ceremony. Each year brought me closer to the time when I would be seated on the freshly cut grass of Navy/Marine Corps Memorial Stadium with my classmates . . . hearing the pronouncement of the president . . . tossing my cover into the air with my buddies and yelling for joy and hugging everyone and having the ensign's shoulder boards snapped onto my uniform. Every year it became more real, more possible to believe in. And 1994 would have been my year. I should have been there right then, sitting with the winners. Instead . . .

I remember going to Angie's television, trying to find something, anything to jerk me out of my tailspin. A game show, a soap opera, whatever. I clicked on the set and the first words I heard, even before the picture formed on the screen, were, "Later today: a live report from the Naval Academy on today's graduation ceremony—" I jabbed the "off" button like the eye of my worst enemy. There was no escape from the misery—not for me . . . not that day.

I'd been labeled a cheater. I'd been found in violation of the Honor Concept, the most sacred tenet of the Brigade of Midshipmen. The Navy determined I was incapable of developing "the proper sense of personal honor required of a commissioned officer."

The shame scalded my insides like an acid bath—and not only because of the personal humiliation. What I was going through was bad enough, but what was all this doing to my family? I'd also cast a shadow on them—on Dad . . . and Grandpa.

My grandpa is a retired Navy captain. His service record reads like a list from some Navy Hall of Fame: the U.S.S. Toledo, the York-town, and the Sacramento. Grandpa was on destroyers during World War II, serving under such legends as Admirals Cobb, Zumwalt, and Clarey. My graduation from Annapolis would have been an endorse-ment of my grandfather's life—a completion of the circle.

When I used to go to Grandpa's on leave, I wouldn't dream of showing up out of uniform. The look on his face when he'd see me was like Christmas morning and a winning lottery ticket, rolled into one. He loved taking me to lunch with his country club friends. Though Grandpa was always a pretty reserved guy, he'd introduce me to people he'd barely met. "Hey, Pete! I want you to meet my grandson, Jeff. He's about to graduate from Annapolis, you know. . . ."

Grandpa had bought airline tickets a year in advance to make sure he was present when I threw my cover in the air. He told me one day during my third year at Annapolis that, at my graduation, he planned to present me with the dress sword he had carried proudly for over thirty years of distinguished military service. If he had told me he'd just distilled his soul into a diamond bottle and placed it in my hands, I wouldn't have been more awestruck. Grandpa's sword! The sword my dad didn't want . . .

Since Grandpa was a captain, Dad had an automatic appoint-ment to Annapolis; all he had to do was accept it. But he refused. He let his number come up and went into the Army as a draftee. Of course, being his father's son, he couldn't be content to just drift along. He got into Officer's Candidate School and later opted for the gut-bucket grind of the 101st Airborne and the elite Ranger Corps. Even with such a demonstration of Dad's resolve and dedication, I'm not sure Grandpa was ever really reconciled to his son's decision.

Though he didn't carry on the family's Navy tradition, Dad could at least say he served his country with honor. He completed the job he was handed and even went beyond what was required. I'm pretty sure my dad's enthusiasm for my appointment to Annapolis was partly due to his guilt over not following in his own father's footsteps.

But, sitting in that lonely apartment, I felt as if I'd just ripped a fresh wound in Grandpa's heart—a wound I had the power to heal.

I remember Angie's coming into the room and sitting down next to me. I knew she'd been crying; her eyes were red and bruised-looking. Still, she was drop-dead gorgeous—slender, with radiant brown hair and dazzling blue eyes—she could be on the cover of any magazine.

I wanted to say something, wished I could hold her and tell her everything was going to be okay. But the words just wouldn't come.

"Jeff, what are we going to do?" she asked in a wavering voice. "All the plans we've made for the future—what's going to happen to us now?" We had discussed marriage. Angie's sky-blue eyes had shone when I described a military wedding in the ornate chapel at the Yard: the uniforms, the military pomp, the pipe organ pealing an anthem while my buddies created a glittering arch of crossed swords for us to walk beneath.

I had already chosen a ship in San Diego as my first duty station—the U.S.S. Essex: a sleek, newly-commissioned helicopter landing ship. I would be an ensign in the Navy, I would marry the only girl I had ever loved, and life would be sweet.

For at least ten years, the single organizing principle of my life had been my desire to graduate from Annapolis and serve as an officer in the United States Navy. I knew Angie's parents were pleased she had fallen in love with a guy who had goals, who was going somewhere. How do they feel about me now? I wondered. What could I tell this girl whose unswerving trust and genuine caring had literally saved my life? Angie deserved so much. What hope, what reassurance could I give her?

"I . . . I don't know, Angie," I stammered at last in a numb voice. "I did the right thing. We'll be okay—somehow." I prayed to God I could believe it . . .

On the screen is a full-frame shot of Morley Safer as he talks to me and Brian Pirko, my roommate at the Academy. I remember seeing Mr. Safer the first time. He was sitting across the room getting made up and being briefed by an assistant producer. It was a little intimidating to be suddenly in the presence of this man I'd only seen on TV. Intimidating and oddly disappointing. In person, you see all the imperfections and blemishes that the makeup and lighting people work so hard to disguise. But it was still fairly impressive, shaking the hand of a bona fide, Pulitzer-class broadcast journalist.

I remember that when the three of us sat down and began talking, Mr. Safer looked at me and said, "Jeff, tell me a little about yourself. What ever made you want to get into the Naval Academy in the first place?"

What, indeed? I've been wondering about that myself the last few months. But the answer to that and so many other questions begins in another place and time . . .

☆ 2 ☆

BEING GOOD ENOUGH

Spokane, Washington 1983

THE COUNT IS 3 and 2, with one out. The pitcher warily eyes the runner on second, even though in Little League he can't steal unless there is a passed ball or some other such mishap. He goes into his stretch, a twelve-year-old's version of the same moves he has watched on TV as Goose Gossage or Catfish Hunter faced a pressure situation in late innings.

At shortstop, I go into my infielder's crouch, just like Dad has coached me. I know the kid at bat has a tendency to get ahead of the ball; chances are the ball will come to my side of the second base bag if the batter connects.

This has been one of my best games. I'm four for four at the plate and I've batted in three runs. I've been perfect in the field and even turned a double play in the third inning. This team is our arch rival in the league, and if we can hold on to the one-run lead, we'll have clinched the league championship. I can hear the blood singing in my ears, smell the mixed odor of insect repellant and cigarette smoke, the smell that means summer night games. The ball is a white blur as the pitcher delivers. The batter swings and suddenly there is no other sound in the world except the firm *crack!* of a hard-hit baseball. The entire universe boils down to me, my glove, and the path of the ball.

I dive to my left, my glove hand outstretched. The line drive bores for the empty air between me and the second base bag, and somewhere in the back reaches of my mind is the thought that if the ball gets out of the infield, the game is tied. My feet leave the ground, my arm stretches desperately toward the only possible point in space where the ball's trajectory might intersect the path of my glove. I feel a firm *thump!* in the webbing, just before my chest plows into the dirt of the base path. Scrambling to my feet, I realize that the runner has anticipated the play and left the bag, headed for third. With the roar of the crowd an indistinct rumor in my ears, I flick the ball to the second baseman, who is already standing on the bag. Double play! The game is over! We've won!

I whirl around, ignoring the cheers and fist-pumping of my teammates, and look toward the dugout, my arms raised over my head. Dad is there, his coaching clipboard flung to the ground, clapping furiously and yelling joyfully at me. "All right! Way to go, Jeff! Atta boy!"

Out of the dense sound, the only thing I hear is the voice of my father. This is the payoff. I have earned his praise, and all I can feel at this moment is an intense relief. I did it one more time. I was good enough.

Teammates clap me on the back, giving and receiving fives all around. There is the obligatory hand-shaking with the other team—heads ducked, eyes averted—the gathering of the equipment into the big canvas bags, and loading up. Then the drive home.

I'm happy for the victory, happy for my contribution to it. But in the deep places of my eleven-year-old heart, I am already dreading tomorrow because I know the whole process must begin again.

I will raise the bar. There will have to be another challenge, another opportunity to prove myself. Dad will congratulate me on the way I played tonight, and I will bask in the approval, savor it like cold lemonade on a hot afternoon. But it won't last. The warm, good feelings will fade, as they always do, and I'll have to do something else to prove I'm good enough.

Good enough for what? I don't know, can't put the feelings into words. All I know is that for some reason, I feel an irresistible need to continually achieve, progress, improve. It's the only way I can hold the bad feelings at bay. I've never been able to make the good feelings last without some new reinforcement, some greater triumph.

My dad, my older brother, and I all love baseball. Many of our conversations are about great players of the past and present. Dad's idol is Mickey Mantle, because he continually overcame adversity and pain to rise to greater and greater heights. I feel that pain and adversity are my natural enemies. If the Mick could rise above them, then Jeff Gantar can, too.

It's the same in school. I can't accept anything less than A's. I can't allow myself to slough off my schoolwork because that might mean that I wasn't trying to be the best. Every time I take a test, every time I do an assignment, I feel two things: an eager anticipation of success and an absolute dread of failure. Dad sometimes tells a story about when I was in kindergarten. At my elementary school in Wenatchee, Washington, my teacher put "happy face" stickers on very good work, "straight face" stickers on average work, and "sad face" stickers on work that was less than acceptable. One day, Dad says, I came home from school in tears. "I'm sorry, Daddy," I sobbed, "I didn't get a happy face sticker today." He looked in my backpack among my papers and, sure enough, there was a handwriting exercise or something with a "straight face" affixed.

"That's all right, son," Dad consoled. "Everybody gets a straight face sticker once in awhile. It's nothing to be ashamed of."

"Not me!" I growled, shaking my head in fierce determination. "I wanted to be the only kid in my room to get all happy faces. I have to get happy faces from now on!"

There was a dark side to my tenacity—I realize that now. I felt a great need for attention and affirmation, and if I couldn't get it by outstanding performance, I would obtain it by crying or by disruptive behavior. Something inside prodded me constantly to be in control, to be calling the shots. That same hidden drive would often awaken me at night with the bad feelings covering me in a clinging sheet of fear. At these times, I would run crying to my parents' bedroom, climbing between them into the safest place I knew. I didn't learn to effectively channel these indistinct compulsions until sometime during my second grade year, when the crying and disruption gradually faded away, leaving only my fierce, uncompromising competitiveness as a coping mechanism.

Sometime in late elementary or junior high, I decided I wanted to attend the U.S. Naval Academy at Annapolis. I'd heard Grandpa tell about his days in the Navy during World War II and after. Grandpa is second only to Dad in my pantheon. Grandpa has a picture on his wall at his house in Florida—a portrait of himself in his summer dress uniform. The image of that portrait is burned into my mind like an icon. Grandpa has four or five rows of medals and what seems like a mop of gold braid draped over his shoulder. There are other pictures on the wall—pictures of foreign dignitaries autographed to Grandpa, plaques and gifts from all over the world that Grandpa had received during his glittering career. For as long as I can remember, I've been in awe of Grandpa. Sometimes I tried to put my own face in the place of Grandpa's in the portrait. I'd imagine myself standing there, stern and distinguished, admired and respected by important people—even people from other countries! That felt really good to me. I visualized myself in the uniform, wearing the smart white cap with the shiny black bill. I saw myself standing on the tilting deck of a destroyer under full steam, feeling the salt spray wash back against my face. I decided I wanted to be a Navy man, like my Grandpa.

I hoped Dad would want me to go to the Naval Academy. I placed a tremendous value on my father's advice and opinions. Sometimes it seemed funny to me that I never thought much about joining the Army even though my dad had been an officer in the Rangers. Being accepted into the Naval Academy became the best thing I could imagine. Maybe if I could get into Annapolis, the bad feelings would go away and never come back. Maybe at last being good enough would be—good enough.

Being good enough was more than a goal for me. It was a means of survival. It was the only way I could think of to insure the approval and acceptance of those who mean the most to me—the only way to feel safe and right.

At the same time, I don't think I ever really doubted that I was loved. I knew that Mom and Dad loved me because they told me and showed love by their actions. Didn't Dad buy me my very own pitching machine, so I could hone my batting skills? And when the pitching machine malfunctioned, didn't Mom frequently spend hours with me in the backyard, pitching to me? I knew that it was important to her because it was important to me.

Mom and Dad met when they were in high school. Julie and Mark Gantar married while he was in basic training and she watched as he went on to Officer Candidate School, to Airborne/Ranger training at Fort Benning, Georgia, then to Jungle School in Panama. Mark, my older brother, was born in 1967, just before Dad went to Vietnam. Mom always seemed happy taking care of me, my older brother, and baby sister: tossing a plastic ball for me to hit back at her, cheering from the stands at our ball games. Mom was warmth and acceptance and safety. Mom was sanctuary.

And Dad . . . He was my coach, my advisor, my mentor, my image of success. I never started anything without consulting him, and I couldn't imagine going against Dad's wishes. His approval meant everything.

Dad was a businessman. When he got out of the Army as a decorated captain, he entered Central Washington University, in Ellensburg, on the G.I. bill. He finished a degree in business administration and went to work for a company that made and sold skin-diving equipment. In a year or so, he joined Pacific Trail, a sports apparel company, managing the Wenatchee manufacturing plant. Mark Gantar was, like his Navy captain father, an overachiever. When he set himself to a task, he often exceeded his own goals. He had the sort of natural confidence that generated trust. His workers placed such faith in him that when their union contract came up for renewal, he persuaded them to reject it, on the assurance that he would personally see to their best interests. Subsequently, the Wenatchee plant became the most profitable in the company. It came as no surprise when, a short time later, he was promoted to general manager of manufacturing, giving him oversight of the firm's entire manufacturing operation.

When Pacific Trail opted to move all factory operations overseas, Dad structured a buyout of the company's stateside manufacturing facilities. At the age of thirty-seven, he was president and C.E.O. of a corporation with multimillion-dollar revenues.

Though in a position to provide more than a comfortable lifestyle for his family, Mark Gantar would not permit his children to become pampered rich kids. The only exceptions? Sports and academics. Whatever the Gantar children needed for athletics or their studies, they got, no questions asked.

In such an atmosphere, perhaps it was inevitable that my brother and I would become intensely competitive with each other. Despite my brother's five-year advantage in age, I couldn't stand to get beat by him—in anything. I was always fighting him, always going one-on-one with him in my mind. It didn't seem to matter what activity was at hand: snow football, tennis, basketball, sledding—even tag. Anything we did together became a contest.

Sometimes the competition even included Dad. Racquetball was a favorite sport of ours, and sometimes the three-way games of "cutthroat" among Dad, Mark, and me came close to being just that. Once, especially, we were so mad at each other at the end of a game that we all stormed out of the court, refusing to talk to each other for hours afterward.

But for some reason, it all worked. I thrived in the heat of battle. Somehow, the struggle seemed to tell me who I was. I think I always expected life to be tough, and I wanted to be ready. I knew my parents—and Dad, especially—had high expectations for me, and I knew there was a reason. I had no intention of disappointing them—or myself.

Maybe winning so much made it worse when I lost. Girls, for example. As junior high approached and I watched more and more of my friends get interested in dating and even "going steady," I began to wonder why the thought of being alone with a girl was so threatening to me. Being with girls in anything other than a crowd created intense anxiety inside me. Eventually, I learned to avoid such situations and at the same time learned to camouflage my reluctance.

The other major heartbreak of my young life came as I entered high school. Like my father and brother, I fully expected to make the varsity baseball team as a sophomore. I was devastated when I didn't make the cut. My despondency over my failure resulted in a lackluster junior varsity year, but it didn't diminish my desire for ultimate success. I would frequently practice batting in my backyard until my palms were raw and bleeding. I would get to school as much as an hour and a half early to practice before classes. And the next season, I made the varsity squad. About this time I conceived the goal of winning a baseball scholarship to college. Money wasn't the problem: Dad could well afford to send me anywhere I wanted to go. But I wanted to earn my way, to be good enough to get there on my own. I thought it would make Dad proud. I became a proficient switch hitter, knowing this would make me more valuable as a ball player.

My string continued: academic honors, athletic awards in baseball and tennis, increasing popularity with peers and teachers. I had everything going my way. As far as anyone else knew, Jeff Gantar was the very picture of success . . . on the outside. But inwardly, I was still burdened by the nagging notion that there was something missing from me that other people had. I couldn't name what was lacking, but I instinctively felt that if I let up for a single moment, if I relaxed my all-out effort toward perfection, everyone would see that I was really a phony, after all. Worse than a phony, they would see that I was unworthy, defective. That there was something wrong with me.

Sometimes I even felt it in church. When Mom, my brother, and I went to Holy Trinity Lutheran on Sundays, the hymns and Scripture readings and sermons sometimes made me want to hide. We sang and studied about a God who is holy and perfect. I knew automatically that such a God couldn't possibly tolerate a flawed, incomplete person like me. I knew that God expects the very best, and I knew there was no way I could ever be that. From the time I was old enough to remember anything, I remember not wanting to go to church, not being able to apply the songs and lessons and Scriptures to myself. Something within me caused me to shrink away from the light, even though I knew it was good. I felt hopelessly unworthy.

And when I was in church, I'd hear about God forgiving sins and about Jesus dying for our sins, but still I had the nagging feeling that others were much better than I was, and that my sins were much worse. My sins were at the core of my identity. I didn't feel that I was worthy of church. I felt completely naked. I thought that God was looking right at me and that he could see through me.

Not that I didn't have opportunities to learn about spiritual things. My mom was a strong spiritual influence on me, and she never gave up on trying to explain things to me to improve my attitude about church and the Bible. I'd ask her things like, "Why did Jesus have to die on the cross?" and she was very patient and kind. She would answer my questions and explain the Bible to me in a way that I could understand.

And then there was my maternal grandfather, Grandpa Karl Engdahl.

Grandpa Karl grew up as an orphan and struggled hard all his life, but the struggle seemed to make him strong and compassionate, rather than hard and selfish. He was a warm man, and the main thing I remember about him is his habit of writing us long letters on important days, like the first day of school, or graduation . . . or confirmation.

My older brother got a long letter from Grandpa Karl on his confirmation, but I never got to read it. My own confirmation was approaching, and there were two things that kept me going to classes, despite my strongly ambivalent feelings about being there: Mom's insistence (sometimes backed by Dad's clout), and the prospect of that letter from Grandpa Karl.

On the day of my confirmation, after I opened all my presents and cards, I opened Grandpa Karl's letter. There was a lot in it that was tough for a fourteen-year-old kid to understand: advice about depending on God no matter what, about avoiding "reckless" associates, about finding my own path and becoming content with doing my best in everything I tried. I had no idea at the time how prophetic Grandpa Karl's letter would be. I folded it carefully and tucked it inside the front cover of the new Bible I got from Aunt Judy, my godmother, and put the Bible in the corner of my top left desk drawer. I never re-read the letter—or the Bible, for that matter—but that top left drawer became a sort of shrine for me. I would write down my personal goals and dreams and put them in that same drawer, next to the Bible and Grandpa Karl's letter. I didn't feel good enough to personally approach Grandpa Karl's God with my problems and wishes, so I contented myself with placing them in the same drawer.

I couldn't put any of these feelings of inadequacy into words. In fact, I was afraid to express them to anyone because I figured that somehow, by admitting weakness, I was aiding and abetting it. I could never talk to Dad about the bad feelings that wouldn't go away. I was afraid Dad might think I was bad, too. And that would have been my own private version of hell.

So I went on, driving myself to succeed, all the while feeling more and more hollow inside. It was like a ghost from my past was hiding deep within me, reminding me that I could never be good enough. I didn't know where the specter came from or how to exorcise it, but I couldn't quit trying, couldn't get off the treadmill.

Amazingly enough, with all the turmoil inside me, I never had trouble attracting the attention of girls. In fact, most of my friends had begun spending a great deal of time thinking about dating, running the typical adolescent slalom course, from victory to defeat and back.

I enjoyed thinking about girls and even talking about girls. But what no one knew, what I could not admit to even my most trusted friend, was the fact that the actual prospect of physical intimacy produced in me the worst discomfort I had ever known. If a girl approached me in an interested way, I'd break out in a cold sweat; my palms would get moist, my heart would pound, and an unreasonable sense of fear would overwhelm me. The experience was utterly frightening and totally incomprehensible. It became for me another confirmation that something was wrong inside me. But, as always, I couldn't let myself roll over and play dead—couldn't just quit. I knew that my friends weren't having such feelings in their experiences with girls. They told about different feelings—delicious, exciting feelings. I knew I had to find a way to have these same feelings. I knew I couldn't be normal until I did.

☆ 3 ☆

RITES OF PASSAGE

I'T'S SATURDAY NIGHT. I'M staying with a friend, and we've heard that a party is going down about two blocks away. We know liquor will be available, since the kid's parents are out of town. My friend is eager to go. "C'mon, man! Booze! Girls! Hear what I'm sayin'?"

We sneak out of the house and walk to the party. I can hear U2's latest CD throbbing through the walls as we near the party house. When the front door opens, a blast of sound and laughter invites us inside.

I know most of the kids here. I mix into the crowd, laughing and joking. Someone sticks a cold can of beer in my hand. I take a drink, then another.

I feel a slight twinge of guilt as the cold brew goes down my throat. I've never done any drinking other than a few trial sips under parental supervision. In fact, my folks are such health nuts, I've barely tasted processed sugar, much less alcohol.

I know alcohol suppresses anxieties and inhibitions, and I persuade myself that a few drinks might actually be good for me.

Circulating among the partyers, I soon realize that I've almost finished the can, and I begin to feel a pleasant buzz. I decide to drink another beer.

A girl comes up to me. I know her; we've been friends since junior high. "Hi, Jeff. What's up?"

"Hey, not much. What's up with you?"

It's never been difficult for me to find girls to talk to. The tough part has always been finding something to say. For all my outward confidence and success, I feel really shy, especially with girls. Especially one-on-one. But I know I must conquer this fear in order to be like my friends. For some reason, they show none of my shyness around the opposite sex. Some of them even brag about their sexual conquests. Something inside me is repelled by such talk, but I can't afford to let anyone sense my distaste. The boasters seem to enjoy the approval of our peers, so their feelings must be the normal ones. More than anything, I want to feel I'm normal.

The grapevine says this girl likes me. Maybe that's why I've avoided her in school and at other gatherings. But with the beers nudging me on, I decide to let things go their own way for a while, see what happens. It'll be okay, I tell myself. Just relax.

We talk for a while. Actually, she does most of the talking. I manage an occasional reply, but I allow her to guide the conversation. "It's getting kinda stuffy in here," she says. "Wanna go outside?"

"Yeah, sure," I hear myself say, almost instantly regretting it. We work our way through the crowd to the front door and go out into the cool air.

My heart is running wind sprints as I walk with her down the sidewalk. She chats amiably, either unaware of my mumbled replies and long silences or too considerate to comment. When we reach a wooded lot, she turns off the sidewalk. Not knowing what else to do, I go with her. There's a small clearing, and she sits down, leaning comfortably against a tree.

I try to restart the stalled conversation, but she isn't interested in talking any more. She's looking at me, her eyes half-lidded, her lips parted. She leans toward me and kisses me. I feel her palm on the back of my neck, pulling me in. Her lips are warm and soft, shaping themselves around my mouth.

A minor riot breaks out, starting in my chest and working its way down from there. A pretty nice riot, at first. I want to enjoy this moment, try to submerge myself in it. This girl is a friend, after all. She wouldn't want to do anything that would hurt me, would she? I tell myself that the bad feelings will go away if I don't let my mind run away with me. I respond to her affectionate advance. The fuzziness in the center of my head mutes the alarm signals that would normally make me hit the "eject" button. It'll be okay, I tell myself, trying desperately to make myself believe it.

But it doesn't work. Even though she has responded enthusiastically to my fumbling advances, I know I can't maintain the façade any longer. Even with the alcohol suppressing them, my fears are rapidly gaining control, and I can't keep going. She pulls back and looks at me, a puzzled expression on her face. "What's the matter, Jeff? Did I do something wrong?"

My face feels like a three-alarm blaze. Choking with embarrassment, I close my eyes and lean my head against the rough bark of an oak tree at my back. "No, you didn't. You didn't do anything wrong at all . . . It's just—I don't know, I guess I just started feeling . . . a little sick, maybe . . ."

"You don't feel good?"

I latch on to the lie, hoping desperately it will bail me out of this monumental mistake I've made. "Yeah, I'm really sorry, but . . . Maybe I had too much beer or something. I guess I'm gonna need to go back, if you don't mind."

The silence is a trifle too long. "No, that's . . . that's okay. I mean, if you feel sick, then we should go."

Unable to look at her, I get up and straighten my clothing. Walking back to the house, I feel her eyes boring into the side of my face. I can't make even the pretense of conversation now, and she's not very talkative, either. I walk her to the door and force myself to give her a chaste peck on the cheek. We go inside, and I'm grateful for the camouflage of noise enfolding us.

As soon as I can, I find my friend and persuade him that I need to leave. We walk back to his house. I'm glad for the darkness, so my friend can't see the humiliation on my face. I make small talk as we go, but the words don't register in my mind until my friend says, "Hey, I saw you leave with Marla. How'd it go?"

Panic! Two steps, then four. "Great," I snicker at last, and roll my eyes meaningfully, hating myself for the lie. "She practically crawled all over me." He wants to know more, but I blow him off with some gonzo line about being a pervert.

How can I tell him the truth? "It was awesome, man. She was as hot as a five-dollar Rolex and I got scared, so I kissed her on the cheek and brought her back to the house. Any more questions?"

Yeah, right. Shame chews my insides like a hound after an old bone. More than ever, I am crushed by the knowledge that whatever normal may be, I'm not it.

I became adept at living two lives at once: the outer, successful life that my peers saw and admired; and the inner, agonizing life with a void at the center that no athletic victory, no test grade, no achievement could fill. The contradiction between the outer Jeff Gantar and the inner was growing each day, and I knew it. I sometimes felt I was living with a black hole inside me; that the emptiness would continue pulling in more and more of me, requiring more and more energy to conceal, until one day I wouldn't be able to continue any longer, would simply collapse upon myself, a vacant, hollow shell. I dreaded the day when I would be unable to maintain the skillful charade, but I didn't think I had a choice. I had to keep raising the bar. I thought that if I kept moving, kept the wind whistling in my ears, I'd be able to drown out the dark voices that haunted me from inside.

☆   ☆   ☆

IN DECEMBER OF MY senior year, the staff of U.S. Representative Tom Foley began conducting screening interviews of seniors in the Congressman's district. Their aim was to surface the handful of outstanding students who might be considered for appointments to the United States armed forces academies at West Point, Colorado Springs, and Annapolis. They interviewed some fifty seniors, of whom they selected five or six finalists. The top finalist would receive an unqualified recommendation for appointment and the others received qualified recommendations. I applied to be interviewed. It was time to see if my dream could come true.

I decided not to inform Grandpa of the interviews and I didn't mention his Naval service in my application. If I got in, it had to be on my own merits, not because of Grandpa's record or influence.

When I applied, my high school counselor was surprised. "Jeff, you've only applied to the Naval Academy, not West Point or Colorado Springs."

"Yes, Sir, that's right."

He leaned back in his chair and looked at me. "Why? Everybody applies at all the academies. It increases your chances of getting an appointment somewhere. Besides, Navy is probably the toughest of the three. In fact, I don't remember any student from University High School ever going to Navy."

"I'm not interested in going anywhere but Navy. I don't see why I should apply anywhere else."

He studied me for what seemed like a long time. I tried to keep my eyes steady on his face, and I remember clenching and unclenching my jaw. "Okay," he shrugged, finally. "Navy it is, then." He held out his hand. "Good luck, Jeff. If anybody can do it, I guess you can."

"Thank you," I smiled, shaking his hand as I got up to leave. "I sure hope so."

After what seemed an eternity of waiting, I was notified that I had received one of the qualified recommendations. Dad and I contacted the baseball coach at Navy, who in turn called my high school baseball coach. Coach Ressa really liked me, and I knew it. I hoped he would say something to Navy that might leapfrog me over the dozens of other athletes vying for a Navy sports scholarship. I was on fire to get in the Academy, and I still dreamed of earning my own way with a scholarship of some sort. Those were the moments of truth. The hours spent with blood-slicked palms in front of the pitching machine, the days of getting up before sunrise to practice before school had finally come down to this. I hoped and prayed my efforts would count for something. I hoped it would all be good enough.

It was. Navy made me their top recruit for baseball. This, in addition to my qualified recommendation and good grades got me an appointment to the United States Naval Academy in May of my senior year.

When the package bearing the imprint of the U.S. Naval Academy arrived at my house, I could barely control my fingers enough to open it. Tossing the cover letter aside, I ripped into the small presentation box containing my certificate of appointment. My heart was going like a triphammer as I stared at the ornate lettering and read the words declaring my acceptance. "Congratulations on your receipt of an offer of appointment to the United States Naval Academy, Class of 1994 . . ."

I stopped reading, unable to move or speak. My eyes must have been wide as saucers, and I remember my mouth moving, but no sound coming out. I jumped up and down like some little kid with his first bike. My family was ecstatic, electrified. It was the absolute best moment of my life. I had won.

Still in a daze, I stumbled to a telephone. I dialed Grandpa's number. "Hello?" crackled the voice at the other end.

"Grandpa? It's Jeff. I've got some good news."

"Hi, Jeff. What is it?"

"Grandpa, I got an appointment to the Naval Academy."

Stunned silence.

"You what? Jeff, I . . . I didn't even know you'd applied!"

"Well, I didn't tell you because I didn't want you to know unless I got in, and I did!"

"Jeff, that's just fantastic! I . . . I don't know what to say!"

The pride in Grandpa's voice was as plain as if he were standing in front of me. I felt as if my grin must have been a mile wide. I had made them all proud.

As the end of the school year approached, I was riding high. I had my Annapolis appointment in hand, I had had an outstanding year in school, I was All-State in baseball. Things had never been better.

But the senior prom was looming, and I had to decide what to do.

Several girls had let it be known that they would be happy for me to ask. But, as always, the thought of being responsible for an entire evening in the close company of an interested female had me looking for the emergency exit. Looking back, I must have been pretty popular, despite my painful shyness. But I could not, for the life of me, summon the nerve to get a date for the prom.

My best friend wanted to double-date to the prom. He had the whole thing set up. We were going to take our prospective prom dates to this nice restaurant in Spokane. I was going to ask my date, who also happened to be a good friend of the girl he was with. As soon as I asked her, he was going to ask his date. "It's a layup," he assured me. "She wants to go with you, and if she does, we'll all go together. It'll be great."

But I couldn't do it. Every time I'd try to get the words out of my mouth, my throat would just sort of clamp shut. I must have looked like a beached bass, the way I kept opening and shutting my mouth. Everybody kept looking at me with this awkward, confused expression—like I'd committed some weird social mistake, like I'd belched out loud at a White House dinner or something. And so, because of me, the double date didn't come off—either that night or at the prom. My friend was too kind to embarrass me and my date by asking his girlfriend in front of us.

On the night of the senior prom, when all my friends were socializing and dancing and creating fond memories of their last days in high school, Jeff Gantar—Annapolis appointee, outstanding athlete, honor student—was at home watching television with his family. Some night to remember.

A week or so later, at commencement, Mr. Manfred, my calculus teacher and the senior advisor, was reading the list of seniors who had received college scholarships and other awards. When he announced my acceptance into Annapolis and my baseball scholarship, my classmates and their families broke into spontaneous applause. I cherished the sound of those cheers, trying to fix the glad noise forever in my mind. I suspected that in the weeks just ahead, I'd need the strength it gave me.

☆ 4 ☆

PLEBE YEAR

June 1990 – May 1991

T HE ELECTRIC SHEARS FEEL cold as they glide over my skull. My hair cascades to the floor, mingling with the multi-hued drifts of hair from the hundreds of new arrivals who had sat in the chair before me. The buzzing of the shears is deafening; seven other Navy barbers are working in unison, shaving the heads of one plebe after another. They will shave over a thousand heads today.

Before coming to Annapolis, I had gotten a haircut at home. I had the barber shave my head really close on the sides, but I asked him to leave a little length on the top, no more than an inch or so. I thought that would be good enough. This wouldn't be the last time I'd underestimate what the Academy could dish out.

I arrived at the Yard on a bus that had met my plane at Baltimore/Washington International Airport. The bus was crammed with guys like me; kids from all over the country with scared eyes and fire in their guts; kids who, like me, had but one purpose: to earn the insignia of ensigns in the United States Navy. Friendships formed instantly. It was a little like being on the same baseball team headed for the state championships. The atmosphere crackled with apprehension and excitement. None of us knew what to expect, but we all knew that what lay ahead would define us forever. There were two possibilities: success or the unthinkable.

After our heads are shaved, they herd us into Halsey Field House for uniform issue. I vaguely envy the female plebes. At least their heads don't look like peeled potatoes.

Yesterday, when I arrived, an upperclassman showed me to my room. As we walked, he told me how lucky I was to be there, how great the Academy was. Just before he left, he said, "I'm not like most of the other upperclassmen here. I don't mind being nice to plebes." I thought about that. What were they going to do to us? How bad could it be? I'd heard stories . . .

As I go through the lines and get my gear, I notice a few upperclassmen standing around, looking at me and the other plebes. They don't say much to us, but they seem to be talking among themselves, like judges at a cattle show, or—like inmates at a prison, checking out the newcomers. I've seen something like that look in sports, at tryouts. The experienced players look that way when they size up the kids coming out for the first time. "Which one of these guys am I gonna have to take out?" the looks say. "Who's vulnerable? Which ones can I intimidate?" I'm pretty sure that whomever the upperclassmen single out won't be getting weekend liberty. I keep my eyes averted, trying to blend into the scenery.

They issue us everything: working uniforms for summer and winter, dress uniforms ditto, shoes, socks, underwear—everything I will wear, use, or touch for the next four years is Government Issue, right down to my toothbrush, soap and toilet paper. It's as if we are to forget our former lives, as if we are now owned, body and soul, by the United States Navy. The old has passed away, and the new has come—ready or not.

When we're all in our whiteworks—the "Cracker Jack"-styled working apparel of the Naval Academy—we assemble in Tecumseh Court, an area in front of Bancroft Hall, our dormitory. There are speeches, brass bands, and more people in uniform than I've ever seen in one place. There are officers with as many ribbons and decorations as my grandfather. And all of them seem to be staring at me, evaluating me. My jaw clenches with determination. I will make it. Not only will I make it, I will excel. I will be the best.

One of the speakers starts telling us we ought to be proud to be sitting where we are, that we are the best and brightest our nation has to offer. He tells us we are future leaders, not only in the military, but in business and in government. He tells us that graduating from the Naval Academy is the key, not just to success, but to greatness. We are the future of the country, he says. We will be senators and congressmen. One of us might even be president. It's happened before. I'm buying it—every bit of it. I want so badly to believe it, want to prove to myself and the whole world that I belong here, that I can be the best of the best. Everything inside me is straining forward, scared witless of what lies ahead, but even more scared of failing to pass the test—whatever form it takes.

As we sit, looking like a lake of Dixie Cups in our round white caps with the plebe's blue rim, there is an ear-splitting roar just overhead. Our faces yank up in amazement as four navy-and-gold F–14 Tomcats scream out of nowhere, almost close enough to touch. The heat from the afterburners nearly singes the hair on my forearms, the roar pounds my eardrums, my chest cavity. As the band strikes up "Anchors Aweigh," the jets catapult upward in a vertical climb, so close to each other they look like a single craft. Suddenly, they peel off in an awe-inspiring starburst display of precision flying. I know I will never forget this moment. I'm really here! The same people who trained these guys to fly will train me to command ships at sea. In this instant, I feel my destiny in the marrow of my bones. I am a Navy man, like my grandfather before me.

Later that evening, I wasn't so sure about my destiny. In fact, I wasn't sure if I was going to live long enough to have one. I was backed against the wall in Bancroft Hall, with an insane upper-classwoman screaming in my face.

The plebes had been ordered to "chop"—to run the halls of our dormitory. Since Bancroft Hall—"Mother B.," as it's affectionately known—is the largest dormitory in the world, this was no small task. We had to run precisely in the center of the hallways, "squaring" each corner as we turned, and shouting "Go Navy, Sir!" as we went. The detailers—upperclassmen who had volunteered to make Plebe Summer a truly memorable experience—screamed at us as we ran by, seizing any perceived irregularity in uniform, gait, or conduct as an opportunity for special, personal attention.

I had no clue why the upperclasswoman had braced me. The first thing I knew, my shoulders were slammed against the bulkhead and she was on me like white on rice. "You miserable plebe scum!" she screamed at me. "You don't deserve to be at the Naval Academy, you maggot!" My eyes felt the size of dinner plates, and a nervous giggle squeezed from between my lips. Big mistake.

A male detailer, standing nearby, immediately leaped into my face. "What are you laughin' at, boy? How'd you like to be laughing out of the other side of your head?" I felt flecks of spittle hitting my cheeks as I stared into the contorted grimaces of the two detailers. I had no idea what to do or say, had no notion what I had done to earn such treatment. It was my first real taste of what the plebe year at Annapolis would be like.

Finally, after screaming every four-letter word in Webster's Unabridged, they let me go. I sprinted to my room, where my roommate, a football player, was catching his second wind. "What happened, man?" he asked as I came in. My face must have looked like I'd just witnessed a chainsaw murder.

"I don't know, it's like—I mean, they're crazy! They're just screaming at us for nothing!"

"Oh, man, it's really startin' now," my roommate replied. "They're gonna be on us all the time from here on."

"What do we do?"

"Just survive, man. Just get through it, somehow."

In these early moments of disorientation, iron bonds of loyalty were forged between classmates. My fellow plebes and I soon learned that the only way to make it was to depend on the group, to cover for each other, and help each other get through the days ahead.

My roommate for plebe summer was John Formoso, a Cuban kid from New Jersey. John was built like a Mack truck, five-eleven and two-fifty plus, shoulders like twin anvils, dark complexion, and the heaviest beard I'd ever seen on a kid my own age. He had attended the Naval Academy Preparatory School, so he already knew a few of the ropes. He was there on a football scholarship. The day I arrived, his gear was already stowed away in our quarters. He helped me a lot, and I pumped him dry of information in those first days. Because John's beard was so heavy, the detailers were always climbing his frame about his appearance. It was really hard for him to get his face and neck to the spic-and-span condition the detailers required, but he busted his tail trying.

Reveille was at 0530, every morning. We had to roll out of our racks, get into workout gear and fall in formation to run to morning workout. Some of the plebes learned a painful lesson about the importance of solidarity with their peers. If a plebe mustered without his roommate, he was punished for "bilging"—making a comrade look bad. Roommates were expected to help each other complete their tasks and get to formation on time. Nobody did anything to cast an unfavorable light on anyone else. "Don't bilge"—it was the cardinal rule of the brigade; it was the key to survival.

Sometimes at formation the detailers would call certain plebes out to recite "rates": nonsense verses and bits of trivia that had to be memorized and regurgitated on command. A detailer might walk up to a plebe and say, "Mister Gantar, how's the cow?" The plebe would be expected to instantly reply, "Sir, she walks, she talks, she's full of chalk. The lacteal fluid extracted from the female of the bovine species is highly prolific in the nth degree, Sir!" There were dozens and dozens of rates, all of which we were expected to know. They had sent us some of this information before we came, in a document called "Reefpoints." I had spent hours back home, memorizing rates and reams of other information we had to know: names and specifications of Naval aircraft and missile systems, chains of command, and tons of other facts and figures.

In addition, we had to learn the names, classifications, dimensions, armament, and characteristics of Naval vessels. Frequently, I ran across familiar names: U.S.S. Sacramento, U.S.S. Yorktown, U.S.S. Toledo . . . Grandpa's ships. Even amid the harsh realities of plebe summer, my dream pulled me onward like a steel filing toward a magnet.

First thing each morning was PEP—Physical Education Program. Chanting cadence, we would jog to Turf Field and begin doing calisthenics. PEP lasted until 0630, and the detailers were always on the alert for any plebe who showed signs of flagging physical stamina. As an athlete, I was in reasonably good condition, but I pitied the guys who weren't. The detailers had all the compassion of Darth Vader, and they saw everything. And if they didn't see something, they'd invent it.

When PEP was over, we had ten or fifteen minutes to go to our rooms, shower and shave, change into the uniform of the day, and report back to morning meal formation at 0700, spotless and creased.

Once, John tried to get by without shaving. Seconds after we fell in, an upperclassman ripped into him. "What's the matter with you, plebe?" he screamed at the barrel-chested, two-hundred-fifty pound football player. "What's that all over your face?"

"No excuse, Sir," John replied, giving the only answer a plebe was allowed in such a situation.

"You didn't shave! You look like crap! You got ten seconds to haul your can back up to your room and get that fuzz off your face!" John sprinted back to our room and grabbed his razor, not taking time to use shaving cream. Thirty seconds later, he huffed back into formation. His face looked like Hamburger Hill. The detailer went right back into him. "What's the matter with you, you idiot?" he screamed. "You're bleeding like a stuck pig! Didn't your daddy teach you how to use a razor?"

"No excuse, Sir."

And this was before breakfast.

The Naval Academy catalogue has this to say about the dining arrangements: "The entire brigade eats at one time in a massive dining area or wardroom, King Hall. Companies sit together and food is served family-style . . ." That's probably true—if your last name is Torquemada or de Sade.

King Hall is the largest dining hall in the world. I don't know how they determined that, but if the Navy says it, it's probably right. I do know that King Hall looks a lot more like an aircraft hangar than a cafeteria. We sat at long tables in the mess hall, and we had to sit at attention, our buttocks perched precariously on the edge of the chairs. Detailers would walk around behind us, measuring the distance between our backs and the edge of the seat. Eyes had to be "in the boat"—locked straight ahead—which made it particularly difficult to serve your plate from the bowls of food which were passed from one rigid-faced plebe to another. We ate "square meals": Each motion of the fork to the plate had to be at perfect right angles, and back to the mouth in the same way. We couldn't look at our plates or our forks, and we certainly couldn't pick up anything that might be dropped. They grill beautiful steaks at Annapolis. Have you ever tried to cut a steak without looking at it?

All the while, detailers were roaming the hall, sometimes demanding that plebes recite rates or ship specs, sometimes

screaming at us for having crumbs of food on our uniforms. The-
oretically, you were supposed to get about 4,500 calories per day,
but no one gained any weight during plebe summer. My roommate
started the summer at 250 pounds, and ended it at 195. My parents were pretty smart, though. They used to send me baby food in
my care packages, because they knew it was high in proteins and
vitamins. Up in my room at night, I scarfed it down like it was
gourmet fare. You had to take any edge you could get.

The first Sunday of plebe summer was my Valley of the Shadow
of Death. Guys had already given up and washed out during that
first week, and I was feeling like doing the same. We went to breakfast that morning, and there was an extra upperclassman at our
table. My squad leader ordered me to "float."

Normally, each table would have about twelve plebes and one
detailer, which was a big help. If there was only one of them and
twelve of you, he couldn't see everything. It took some of the pressure off. But with two detailers there, some plebe had to give up his
normal seat and float—go sit at the table with the battalion commander. I was the only plebe at the table. There was no place to hide.

They were all over me for the entire meal. "What's the matter
with you, Mister Gantar? I asked you to pass me the eggs!" "Gantar, you idiot! You eyeballed me just now! Keep your stupid plebe
eyes in the boat!" "Who was the Secretary of the Navy during the
Eisenhower administration, Gantar? Come on, Mister Gantar, I
asked you a question!" "Mister Gantar, you better watch yourself.
You're never gonna make it at the Naval Academy, son!"

I didn't eat a single bite, and I was starving. I felt like a hunk of
meat in a shark tank. After the "meal," I went back to my quarters,
my emotions in shreds. I felt the despair rising up like a black tide.
I'm not gonna make it! Ten more months of this—there's no way!
I can't take this. Why did I ever come to this place? I cried, I prayed,
I begged the universe for mercy. And then I got squared away and
went to chapel.

Though I was ashamed to admit it to my peers, chapel was an emotional and spiritual refuge for me. For one thing, it was quiet—about the only time during the week you could say that. And, somehow, the solemn atmosphere, the muted light coming through the stained glass windows, the quiet authority of the architecture—it all combined to create an environment of peace and rest. Sometimes in chapel, I remembered Mom and Grandpa Karl, remembered the things they used to tell me about God and his love. Sitting in that place after the chaos of the rest of the week, I could almost allow myself to believe. I could pray and almost believe I was being heard. But I couldn't admit any of these feelings to my classmates. When I headed off to the chapel, I usually told them I was going to jog.

For some reason, I was able to hang in for the next few days, and things seemed to get better. Not like the detailers suddenly got friendly or anything like that. I was able to . . . survive, I guess. Make it from one hour to the next. I think I went into some type of walking coma. I didn't allow myself to think about how long I would have to endure, about the guys who were washing out, about anything except the next thing I had to do, the next obstacle I had to surmount. I was zoned. I was surviving. I was getting through plebe summer the only way I knew how.

We were getting by on six hours of sleep or less every night. The days seemed to last thirty-six hours each.

Plebe summer was divided into two "sets." At the end of July, we got a fresh group of detailers. I suppose you can only deal out a certain amount of abuse before you have to get some rest. Apparently, being on the receiving end doesn't require any compensating R & R.

By the end of the first set, I had earned the designation of "super." I was ranked first in my squad and I got to wear a gold jersey to PEP. Everyone else wore navy blue. The first day of the second set, the new detailer came up to me.

"Mister Gantar, what are you doing with that gold jersey?"

"Sir, I'm a super, Sir!"

"Is that right?"

"Sir, yes, Sir!"

"Who says you're a super, Mister Gantar?"

"Sir, my old squad leader, Sir!"

"He ain't here anymore, though, is he, Mister Gantar?"

A moment of hesitation. "Sir, no, Sir!"

"So you're not a super, as far as I'm concerned, Mister Gantar."

Another long, awkward moment. "Sir, I'm a super, Sir!" If he had ordered me to take off the jersey, I think I'd have puked on his shoes.

He looked at me for a couple of minutes, and I was sweating bullets. Finally, he said, "Tell you what, Mister Gantar. You're going to have to prove to me that you're worthy of that gold jersey. You've gotta earn it from me, too."

"Sir, yes, Sir! I'll do that, Sir!"

The detailers would crowd around me at PEP, yelling at me when I did pushups or situps. "Come on, Mister Super Gantar! Everybody out here is doing fifty pushups! If you're a super, you can do seventy-five! Come on, Gantar!" And I did seventy-five.

We had to run hundred-yard sprints, and I had to be first every time. They'd take turns running beside me, yelling at me. "Hey, Super Gantar! How come I'm keeping up with you, Gantar? That as fast as you can go, you pansy? My baby sister could beat this!" Never mind that while I had been doing my hundred pushups and situps, they were standing around talking and laughing. "Let's go, Gantar! The rest of these clowns are catching up! You're supposed to be first, Mister Super Gantar!" And I was first.

One day, the squad leader told me he had something special planned. "Gantar, today when we run sprints, you have to start behind everybody else in the company. And you have to finish first. Whaddya think?"

"Sir, yes, Sir!"

"Oh, is that right? 'Yes, Sir!'—just like that? Gantar, you can't do it, and you know it!"

"Sir, yes I can, Sir!"

"You'll never make it, Gantar!"

"Sir, yes I will, Sir!" I had to scream the answer to keep from crying.

There were thirty-five in the company, and I had to let all of them leave the line before I could start running. We ran one sprint, and I passed them all. We ran another one, and I did it again. The detailers were screaming at me, trying to distract me, talking trash to me, doing anything they could think of to throw me off. By the time we were halfway through PEP, my chest felt like pounded meat. When I took a breath, I thought I could taste blood.

On the third sprint, another company was running toward us. I had to run between them and my company in order to get around. I was about to pass the last guy, just before the finish line, when I collided with someone in the other company. I was running flat out, pushing for the line with my head down and I never saw him coming. It was like running into a tree; our chests collided and the impact spun me halfway around. My feet came out from under me and the only thing I could see was sky, just before the ground slammed into my back. I hit like a sack of concrete. When I tried to get up, my shoulder felt like I'd been playing "red rover" with a rhino.

They took me to Ambulatory Care and packed my shoulder in ice. I was sitting there, staring like a zombie and sucking air, when my squad leader came in. "Mister Gantar." I looked around and saw him.

"Mister Gantar, you've earned that gold jersey. You're a super." That was it; that was all he said. Then he turned and walked out.

Vindicated! At that moment, my gold jersey meant more to me than a Congressional Medal of Honor.

I pushed myself to the limit. I always tried to do ten percent more than they asked me to do, and slowly, it began to have an effect. My squad leader began noticing, began using me as an example to the other plebes.

One day at "tables" (mealtime) he said, "You guys ought to come out to Bishop [the baseball stadium] and watch Mister Gantar practice. The other day, I saw him double off the left field wall. He's gonna be one of the best players Navy's ever had. And he still finds time to study his rates and specs. You guys have twice as much time as he does, but he's more motivated. If you want to know what it means to give one hundred-ten percent, you ought to come watch Gantar practice baseball."

I would get really embarrassed, but I have to admit—such praise was like cool rain after a long drought. When you go for two or three months and nobody talks to you except in curses and screams, you get hungry for approval—any kind of approval. And after all, I wasn't trying to bilge—to make my buddies look bad. I was just trying to be good enough. It was all I knew how to do. If my squad leader had only known, I was ten times more afraid of failure than I could ever be of him. In a way, the Academy was more predictable than my life at home. Here, they'd always raise the bar for me. All I had to do was clear it. And then they'd raise it again.

We all had counseling sessions with our squad leaders. Usually, these were critiques where they would tell you what areas you needed to work on, where you needed to improve. By the middle of my plebe year, my counseling times had become strategy sessions where my squad leader would ask me what we could do to get the rest of the guys to improve their performance. Because of my performance ranking, I was promoted to training officer for my company. I was responsible for helping the other plebes improve their scoring and performance. As far as my classmates and detailers were concerned, I was gung-ho, committed, totally motivated. I was looking good.

During Plebe Summer, we were introduced to the Honor Concept of the Brigade of Midshipmen. Actually, "introduced" is a shade mild. We were force-fed it, we were immersed in it, we had it crammed in every opening they could find.

The Honor Concept was presented to us as the ultimate standard of a midshipman's character and conduct. As far as the Academy was concerned, it seemed to outrank even the Ten Commandments. One thing about the Honor Concept—it's simple. You can summarize it in two short sentences: "Midshipmen are persons of integrity. They do not lie, cheat, or steal."

The detailers would adopt a reverent, almost prayerful tone of voice when they talked about the Honor Concept. They would explain to us that it wasn't enough just to avoid saying something that wasn't true. Willfully allowing an incorrect impression to remain, intentional concealment of information—that was lying, too. Cheating was more than just sneaking a crib sheet into an exam. Failure to give proper credit for research materials, unauthorized assistance on individual assignments—these constituted cheating. Any wrongful appropriation of property or materials from the rightful owner or diversion of property or materials from the proper use—that was stealing.

It was drilled into us that the Honor Concept was the minimum standard. We were to judge all facets of our lives by its requirements. If we couldn't function acceptably in accordance with it, we could rest assured that we were not "fit to hold a commission in the Naval Service" and might "jeopardize [our] privilege of being [members] of the Brigade of Midshipmen."

The plebes soaked it up like sponges. We had expected the Academy to demand the best, and we viewed the Honor Concept as the ultimate example of the price we were willing to pay to pass muster. We were beginning to understand why greatness was the rule, rather than the exception, for Annapolis graduates. We were altar boys in the Cathedral of Destiny, and we squeezed our blue-rimmed Dixie Cups in sweaty palms and swallowed hard and raised our hands and swore undying loyalty to the Honor Concept. More than anything, we wanted to ascend into the Holy of Holies—to survive the grind and the humiliation, to pass through the purifying fire and one day be transformed into those heroic figures we feared and admired: midshipmen first-class. The Honor Concept stretched upward like Jacob's Ladder. We knew it would be tough, that it would demand from us the very best that we could offer— but we would make the climb or die trying.

And for me, the Honor Concept became a sort of Path to Enlightenment. After all, I had spent my entire life to this point trying to find a way to be good enough. Here, at last, was a sure-fire way, I thought. If I could embody the Honor Concept, if I could be good enough to meet even such a rigorous test as that, then surely I would be able to conquer the bad feelings. I would be whole and fulfilled and unafraid of even the most arduous scrutiny. I would be good enough—even for me.

Of course, the Honor Concept wasn't our biggest problem that first year. With all the organized and informal misery the upperclassmen dealt us, we didn't really have time or energy to get into trouble. Later on, we would come to understand that the Honor Concept was something to be feared: a club they could use to beat you up, a lever they could use to pry you away from the Academy and your chance at greatness. We would learn the most-used option for dealing with the Honor Concept was absolute denial of the appearance of wrongdoing. You had to be adept at camouflage. In other words, "you rate what you skate." But all that was in the future. For now, we weren't primarily concerned about adherence to some ethereal code of military ethics. We were more worried about making it to the next day without a nervous breakdown.

The first of September approached with the inevitability of an armed invasion. During Plebe Summer, the ratio of upperclassmen to plebes was about one to five or six. In September, when the upperclassmen got back from their summer fleet assignments, it would become three of them for every one of us. No wonder their first night back was called Hell Night. You would think the "youngsters"—the new midshipmen third-class who had been plebes the year before—would be the worst. With memories of plebe year still fresh, you'd expect them to be more than eager to do unto others what had been done unto them. In fact, we feared the second class far more, since it was their specific job description to persecute the plebes. The firsties were sort of above all that. Their main job was to supervise the mayhem visited upon us by the second class. The youngsters were actually supposed to help us all they could. Some did—most didn't.

The thought of Hell Night was like the feeling you get when you know you're going to be sick to your stomach. You aren't sick yet, but you're gonna be—no way around it. And the feeling just grows and grows and you can't do anything except wait for it and wish it didn't have to happen, but it's coming and you know it and you can't do anything but wait. That's what the thought of Hell Night is like.

Parents' Weekend is at the end of the summer just before the academic year begins. My mom, dad, and sister flew out from Spokane to see me. They could hardly believe the change in their Jeffy Boy. I had never been a particularly impolite kid, but by this time I was "Sir"-ing and "ma'am"-ing everything in sight. They could sense the stiffness and tension that possessed me anytime an upperclassman came into view. But even at that, being with my family was like a vacation at Disneyland compared to my life at the Academy. They took me out to a Mexican restaurant in Annapolis, and it felt so good to talk and laugh at a meal, to look around wherever I liked, to relax and even put my elbows on the table if I wanted to.

I'll never forget how desolate I felt when they took me back to Bancroft Hall on Sunday evening, just before they left to go home. The plebes knew the returning upperclassmen were going to nail us that night, and the nine months until our deliverance stretched before us like a hallway in Freddy Krueger's funhouse.

Standing at the doorway with my family, I could hear the upper-classmen inside, screaming at my buddies. Looking into the loving, compassionate faces of my parents and my sister, I felt the tears welling up. My dad told me later that leaving me that day was about the hardest thing he'd ever done. When I turned away from them and walked into Mother B., it was perhaps the loneliest moment of my life.

Those days are a blur. I remember bracing against a bulkhead, shoving my chin against my sternum and screaming "Yes, Sir! No, Sir!" until a raw whisper was all I had left. I remember doing millions of pushups and situps, memorizing dozens of birthdays and girlfriends' names. Anything they asked us to know was fair game. We had to know how many days it was until we were promoted from plebes to youngsters, how many days until the second-class midshipmen's Ring Dance, how many days until first-class graduation, how many days until the next Army-Navy athletic contest . . . you name it. An upperclassman would come up to you and say, "Mister Gantar, what are the days?"

"Sir, eighty-six days until the Army-Navy football game, Sir; two hundred seventy days until we climb Herndon, Sir; two hundred seventy-one days until Ring Dance, Sir; two hundred seventy-five days until graduation, Sir!" If he had asked you to memorize the days to his birthday or some other personal date, you had to rattle that off, as well.

And then he might ask, "Mister Gantar, who was President Kennedy's press secretary?"

"Sir, I don't know, Sir!"

"Find out, Mister Gantar. Next time I see you, you better know."

"Yes, Sir! I will, Sir!" And I would spend an hour in the library, finding out the answer to his question. Then I could work on my class assignments.

Nestled into the main part of each day was a little thing called academics. While you endured the blood, sweat, and tears of plebe year, you couldn't afford to forget that the United States Naval Academy is also jealous of its reputation as a highly-respected scholastic institution. The faculty, top to bottom, is made up of some of the most outstanding professors in the country, and most classes were anything but easy.

A plebe is expected to complete sixteen credit hours each of his two semesters. There are no elective courses; a plebe takes what he's told. Calculus I and II, chemistry, rhetoric and literature, computer science, Naval engineering—these are part of the core curriculum that each midshipman must pass in order to graduate.

Professors didn't seem to care much about what went on before and after class—which, of course, was what a plebe spent most of his time thinking and worrying about. We were expected to do at least the same amount and quality of work as any other college freshmen, in addition to PEP, military training, and the normal, unrelenting torment by the upperclassmen. On top of all that, I had baseball practice every day after classes. There was a news story that mentioned how one guy's hair fell out during his plebe year, then grew back in—white as snow. The guy was eighteen or nineteen years old, remember. That was what plebe year could do to you—if you could stick it out at all.

A few times during plebe year, I thought about my secret abnormality. I remembered my disastrous experiences with girls; I wondered when I was ever going to have time to work on my problem. But I just didn't have the energy to do anything about it. Plebe year was taking everything I could scrape together just to survive. I buried these thoughts as deeply as I could and tried to appear like every other scared, obedient plebe in the Yard.

Spring finally started to arrive; the days until graduation and promotion were into double digits: eighty days, sixty days, forty days. We started to believe that we could actually make it to the end of our plebe year, that we would actually climb the Herndon Monument and become youngsters. Somehow, we had hung on. Even though the upperclassmen were still screaming at us and bracing us and calling us dirtbags and dog puke and worse, we could begin to imagine life beyond plebe year.

☆   ☆   ☆

THE HERNDON MONUMENT IS a granite obelisk, similar in shape to the Washington Monument. Fortunately for plebes, it's only about thirty feet high.

The final rite of passage for plebes is the ritual scaling of Herndon. Since the preceding July we had counted down the days to this event that officially marked our passage from lowly plebes to third-class "youngsters." On the Friday of Commissioning Week—five days before graduation—we surged around the spire like a lynch mob, insane with the nearness of our deliverance from bondage.

Prior to the assault, the upperclass covers the Herndon monument with a two-to-three inch coating of high-quality lard, placing a plebe's "Dixie Cup" on the very top, then securing it with tape, rope, glue—anything they can think of. The plebes' objective is to remove the Dixie Cup and place an officer's combination cover on the point of the spire. Competition to actually drop the cover on top of Herndon was keen: tradition holds that the person who performs the deed will be first in the class to make admiral.

We mustered at noon that day in Tecumseh Court, the same place where we had listened to the speeches on the first day of Plebe Summer, the place where we had taken the midshipmen's oath of office. This was the absolute last time the upperclassmen could brace us and harass us, and they took full advantage. They were in our faces from the get-go.

There were even a few guys in my class who, for various reasons, had drawn extra, last-minute attention from the upperclassmen. Guys who weren't worthy of promotion, in the opinion of the upperclassmen. They had some of them out at the crack of dawn that morning, doing uniform races. In a uniform race, you had to report in one uniform—say, your choker whites—then, in less than a minute, go back to your room and change into your service dress blues, creased and buttoned down. Then into your whiteworks. Then into your black work uniform. And so on, and so on, until the upperclassman got tired of playing with you or you broke down. No one got immunity, even on the morning of the day we climbed the monument.

Thirty-five or so of the guys who had started the year weren't in our class anymore. Five plebes from my own company had dropped out. I don't think we talked about them much, other than in murmurs of regret that they had "lost it." The unspoken assumption was that they had lost their shot at destiny, that they had fallen off Jacob's Ladder. Too bad, we thought. The other unspoken assumption, following hard on the heels of the first, was, It won't happen to me. I'm gonna make it. I'm going to the top of the ladder.

There's always a crowd on Herndon day gathered around to watch the spectacle. The signal for the assault on the monument was the firing of a cannon. It went off, and over nine hundred plebes broke formation and ran to the monument, screaming like attacking Zulus.

We surged forward, hoisting our comrades onto our shoulders, creating a human scaffold. The guys who stood in the lower tiers had to link arms around Herndon to gain enough stability to support the next layer of climbers. After a while, the obelisk looked like a sugar cube in the center of an ant bed, completely sheathed in a heaving, swarming mass of shouting, sweating plebes. The guys at the top had to try and maintain their balance on the sweat-slicked, lard-speckled shoulders of their classmates. There are falls every year. Sometimes a whole layer of climbers will just collapse, folding down into the melee. I guess the only reason no one's ever been seriously hurt is that there is such a crush of humanity to provide a cushion. Besides that, you're on such an adrenaline high at that point that a fractured ribcage wouldn't register much more than a mosquito bite.

One of us—I honestly can't remember who—finally wriggled within an arm's length of the top and ripped off the Dixie Cup. Then he put the cover in its place. We roared till our throats were raw. It was over. The year of nonstop subservience and strain was over. We were youngsters. We were really on our way.

☆ 5 ☆

YOUNGSTER
YEAR

May 1991 – June 1992

I WAS ASSIGNED TO YPs for my first summer cruise duty. YPs—"Yard Patrol Craft"—are 100-foot boats used for sea training of midshipmen. They have wooden hulls and are basically miniature versions of regular Naval craft. The main areas on board are the bridge, the CIC (Command Information Center), the mess and the berthing, where everybody sleeps. A YP would usually be commanded by a lieutenant with maybe a lieutenant JG (junior grade) just under him. There would be a couple of first-, second-, or third-class petty officers—noncommissioned officers—an enlisted seaman or so, and about thirty midshipmen. Eight or nine of the mids would be firsties and would act as officers on board. The rest would be youngsters, and our function was about the same as the enlisted men. I was assigned to helm and lee helm duty, which meant that I was responsible for manning the engine control in the bridge.

Our cruise left the Yard in mid July, and our itinerary sounded pretty exciting: Boston, Halifax, Nova Scotia, and Prince Edward Island on the outbound leg, then Newport and New York City on the way back. We'd usually spend four or five days at sea, followed by two or three days in each port.

The summer cruises are intended to provide practical application for the lessons learned at the Academy. The idea is to place midshipmen in actual nautical situations and begin teaching them how to function as a crew—how to depend on each other and follow orders and carry out the responsibilities of managing a ship at sea. It was the next rung on the ladder, the next step toward the Holy of Holies. I imagine the regular Navy views the YPs as bikes with training wheels, but for me it was pretty thrilling to be in a real crew on a real boat on a real ocean.

Maybe the best thing about my youngster cruise was getting to be friends with Brian Pirko. Brian and I were in the same company during plebe year, but with everything that was going on, we didn't exactly have time to get well acquainted. We were on different crews during youngster summer, but we were in the same ports several times during the month-long cruise period. We got to know each other and began to realize we had a lot in common. I think it was during the youngster cruise that we decided to be roommates during the academic year. Brian and I stayed together for the next three years—through everything that happened. You don't find friends like that very often in a lifetime, but Brian's that kind of friend.

I think it was during my youngster summer cruise that I began to notice chinks in the armor of my awe for the Honor Concept. At first it wasn't anything earthshaking. For example, it was pretty common for the firsties—who were over twenty-one—to buy booze in port for some of the youngsters, who were mostly underage. Now, the Academy handbook says that drinking is to be handled with moderation and is forbidden to underage mids, but the Naval Academy doesn't enforce that rule with any level of consistency. Two-for-

Seven Night is a good example. That's when the firsties sign the documents committing them to their tours of duty. That's also when the Academy brings in the beer trucks, taps scores of kegs, and watches beatifically as the new gladiators proceed to drink themselves into oblivion. Sometimes the party even spills out into Annapolis proper; bar fights and the ensuing property damage have sometimes reached epic proportions on Two-for-Seven Night. But after all, we were young warriors on our way up the ladder! Weren't we entitled to blow off a little steam now and then? And, hey, the firsties wanted the youngsters to know they were human, too. Just a little innocent fun among the Best and Brightest, right? It wasn't really the same thing as lying or cheating, and the hooch was all bought and paid for.

And as for the abuse of rank, well . . . that sort of went with the territory, didn't it? It was understood that if you didn't want to do a distasteful job, you gave it to someone of lower rank. And if it was really distasteful, you gave it to someone you didn't like of lower rank. And if you did that enough times and the unliked, lower-ranked person got fed up and told the Navy to shove it, well . . . That was just the way things were done, right? You prune the dead wood and improve the tree, right?

But, somehow, it didn't chime true with the Religion of the Honor Concept into which we'd been initiated as plebes. Somehow, this kind of behavior didn't seem to exactly fit with the austere ethics the Honor Concept demanded. It wasn't a big deal . . . but it was the beginning.

By the midpoint of the cruise, most of the youngsters on board were feeling pretty cocky. None of us had experienced the dire nausea we were told we could expect on the way to acquiring our sea legs. We had all decided we were plenty salty enough for anything the Atlantic could dish out. Some of the guys made the mistake, early in the cruise, of utilizing skin-absorbed motion sickness patches. We quickly dubbed such paraphernalia "wimp wedges." If you were a real salt, you didn't need wimp gear like that.

And then came the Night of the Reappearing Pasta.

We were underway toward Newport from a layover in St. John's, Newfoundland. At mess that evening we had all eaten prodigious amounts of pasta shells stuffed with cheese and smothered in tomato sauce. Able-bodied seamen like us had to keep up our energy, and we dug in like lumberjacks.

And then we steamed right into the middle of a summer storm on the North Atlantic. The waves tumbling toward us looked like liquid skyscrapers. The 100-foot YP tossed around like a cork in a Jacuzzi. Even the saltiest youngster among us had not reckoned with the possibility of a real live storm. Within minutes, we were barfing like backed-up toilets. If I hadn't known I'd eaten pasta with red sauce just before, I'd have thought I was tossing up my innards. And even when my gut was empty, I still had the dry heaves.

We tried to man our stations, but it was no use. There wasn't enough time left over between trips to and from the side of the bridge to do any useful work. By the end of the night, the regular officers and enlisted seamen were running the ship. The youngsters were all lying on the floor in the berthing, unable to move. Every once in a while, some playful firstie would stroll into our area and nudge one of us with his toe. "C'mon, man, get up! You're okay! Just a little seasickness, that's all it is! Get up and do some work!" We just adored such little witticisms. Our only regret was that we were too weak to demonstrate our appreciation. All we could do was lie there and swear at them in our heads. I don't think I got off my back for two whole days.

We finally dropped anchor in Newport. Leaving the boat, we noticed a red stain down the side below the bridge. I'm not sure what they use to get tomato sauce off the side of a ship. My first stop was the nearest pharmacy. There was already a long line of mids in front of me—buying wimp wedges.

It was soul stirring to stand on the bridge of the craft as we entered New York Harbor, to stare up from sea level as the Statue of

Liberty slid by like a gigantic parade float. It was like being tele-ported into the middle of a picture postcard or a history book. And when we steamed back into the Yard at the end of the cruise, I felt like a knight returning from a crusade.

I knew that there were about a thousand kids who were, right then, sweating and grunting and bracing and "Yes, Sir"-ing their way through Plebe Summer, and I knew without a doubt that between me and them there was a great gulf fixed. I had stood on the bridge of a vessel and carried out the responsibilities of an active-duty seaman; I had tasted the fear and nausea of a storm at sea; I had laughed and eaten and showered and lived cheek-by-jowl with fifty guys for a month on a 100-foot boat and had done my job and done it well. I had tasted the salt spray. I knew the shape of my future—it was only a matter of time.

The difference between plebe year and youngster year is the dif-ference between being a garbage truck and a family sedan. As a youngster, you aren't required to brace or do any of the demeaning things that make plebe life so special. You don't have to muster nearly so much, don't have to be at the beck and call of any detail-ers. You can sit almost normally in King Hall and actually look at the food you're eating. All you have to do is maintain your acade-mics and not cross the conduct officers, firsties, and second-classes.

Before the academic year began, I agonized over one decision. I came to the conclusion I had to quit the baseball team.

It wasn't that I'd had a bad year on the team, even as a plebe. I had batted .400, and I was getting better and better as a leftie. I knew I had a better than average shot at being the starting second baseman as a youngster.

It was like deciding which finger to cut off. On the one hand, baseball was the passion I'd inherited from my father. My earliest def-initions of success were framed in terms of RBI's and batting averages.

On the other hand, I knew I wasn't getting any closer to a solu-tion to my secret problem. On youngster cruise, I'd been reminded again that real men didn't get scared around interested women. Now that I wasn't a plebe anymore, I'd have more liberty, more chances to meet girls. I needed to figure out why I didn't tick like everyone else. Even more than success in baseball, I wanted success in life. I defined success, at least in part, as attaining a feeling of normalcy. I'd had a good home life, a good family. I wanted the same things someday. But I knew I'd never have them as long as I was too scared of women to be able to experience intimacy.

I had to find time to explore the mysteries inside myself, and something had to go. Baseball was it.

I wasn't exactly sure how to tell my coach—so I didn't. I just didn't show up for the first team meeting. I got a note from him instructing me to turn out for practice. I told one of my former teammates that I wasn't going to be playing anymore. And that was approximately when the organic fertilizer came in contact with the rotating blades on the ventilating machine.

My coach was outraged, and I can't really blame him—out of the clear blue, he'd just lost someone he was counting on for the upcoming season. My teammates were shocked and upset. I'm sure they felt betrayed. You have to understand that no one had any warning whatsoever that I was quitting. I had always given 110 percent in practices and in games. Not to mention that quitting—anything—was not on anybody's "top ten" list at the Naval Academy. It just wasn't in the vocabulary. Midshipmen don't lie, cheat, steal—or quit. Quitters don't ascend Jacob's Ladder.

But I felt I had no choice.

☆   ☆   ☆

AS THE ACADEMIC YEAR progressed, the constant experience of double standards became impossible to ignore.

As a plebe, there are no contradictions—you're dog food all the time and you know it—every day, all year long . . . no problem. For a plebe, life is very predictable. You don't expect much, and you're never disappointed.

As a youngster, however, you get a chance to get your face out of the dirt long enough to start looking around. You begin to see that certain classes of mids—football players, especially—get better privileges, easier classes and best of all, better gouge.

Gouge is the coin of the realm at Annapolis. Midshipmen are under tremendous pressure to make grades. The required courses are difficult and the professors are not known for their leniency, in most cases. Gouge is anything that can be used to prepare for an exam. Old exams, class notes, study guides, practice problems— you name it. If it helps and it's available, it's gouge. There is good gouge and there is better gouge . . . and then there's football gouge— the grade-A, primo, best there is.

To say the football team is privileged is like saying Charles Manson was a little disturbed. First of all, many of them come to the Academy from NAPS—the Naval Academy Preparatory School. Graduating from NAPS with a 2.0 GPA ("C" average) guarantees acceptance into the Academy. Each NAPS graduate costs the taxpayers about $40,000, and the majority of the graduates are headed for the football team when they get to the Yard.

Football players get to register for classes before anybody else, which means they get all the "hook" (easy) profs. My roommate was in an "athletic" section for calculus one semester. He said it was a joke compared to a normal calculus class. Football players were exempted from noon meal formation, and when they did get inside King Hall, they got double portions at tables; sometimes even a completely different—read "better"—menu. They got EI (Extra Instruction) where they got most of their highest-quality gouge. They were exempted from drill and parades. They didn't have to pass the PE tests we did. Some of them—these guys are football players, mind you—couldn't have passed them anyway. Football plebes could hang out in the locker rooms and around the athletic complex and avoid some of the worst hassling by the upperclassmen. Normal plebes had no such protection. Footballers often took their pro quizzes—exams over military protocol, rates, or procedures— late, which in many cases meant after they had gotten the answers from their less fortunate roommates. They had less stringent uniform standards. And nearly every mid has stories of football players whose conduct violations got swept under the rug. There is widespread resentment among the rest of the brigade for the rating and skating of the football team. I'll say this for them, though: they stick together like Elmer and glue. You don't need to worry about any football player bilging another. It's not going to happen—the football team is just about the tightest unit at the Yard. Imagine that.

There were lots of other things that began to bug me besides preferential treatment for football players. For example: a firstie is assigned to do room inspections for the company. He goes into a classmate's room and it's a total wreck—racks are a mess, quarters not squared away, crap everywhere—but he gives the room an "excellent." Then, to soothe his conscience, he goes into a youngster's room and rips it apart—literally. He ditches the room on his inspection report and the youngsters get bad marks on their military conduct ratings. The firsties, on the other hand, rate. Therefore, they skate.

Before long, I began to get the impression that the Honor Concept grades on the curve. I began to have doubts about the guys above me on the ladder.

And then, we began hearing about a thing called "Tailhook."

Some naval aviators at their convention in Las Vegas got a little carried away, it seems: too much to drink, some nonregulation handling of females—fun stuff like that. Pretty soon, a few enterprising reporters got hold of the story and the damage control units kicked into warp drive. To quote a friend of mine in the regular Navy, "sweat pumps were brought on line wide-open and the upper echelons went high and right." The scramble to evade responsibility assumed all the decorum of a feeding frenzy, and the blame ran all the way to the admiralty. The big guys became very interested in covering their sixes and looking righteous.

We had specially called formations where they'd lecture us on the evils of sexual harassment—and not just at the Academy. Stories were rampant in the regular Navy about whole days devoted to this type of training, of hours spent standing at parade rest, listening to the brass harangue everyone about changing their attitudes or having their Navy careers cut short. It went from being a joke to a bore to a major irritation.

At the Yard, our take on the situation was that a few rowdies had created a black eye for the Navy. We knew such behavior was totally out of line, but we just didn't think it typified the majority of Naval officers. As the affair continued to unfold, however, the brass's stories started to sound more and more like so much shuck and jive. Apparently, even the Most Holy Place could be booby-trapped.

☆   ☆   ☆

I DECIDED THE BEST way to figure out how to be a normal guy was to observe mids who were doing it.

Unlike plebes, youngsters get liberty on the weekends. The unstated mission of many youngsters is to get as wasted as possible between sundown on Friday and midnight on Sunday. In fact, there is a tacit expectation that, as a youngster, you will do your dead-level best to make up for all the partying you missed as a plebe. It was a kind of duty. Who wants to shirk duty?

I was a little worried about all the drinking. My dad had warned me to watch out for the guys who boozed too much. He had told me that for many people, the Navy lifestyle involved drinking to excess. I knew he was right, and I wasn't really comfortable going along on the extracurricular forays into the Twilight Zone—but I went anyway.

For a while, it seemed to be working. We would go to a club, often with a classmate who was old enough to buy liquor. We'd get noisy and obnoxious, and our uniforms would draw women. I watched my buddies go through the mating rituals: swapping names and phone numbers, using every pickup line in the book, suggesting private parties of one type or another, handling as much of the goods as they could get away with.

There was one guy—we'll call him Flanagan—who was as shameless as he was inept. He'd slide up beside some cute girl and lay some line on her like, "Yeah, I'm in F–14s. Just got up here on leave from Pax River," referring to the Patuxent River flight test station of *Right Stuff* fame. Now, the women around the Yard aren't stupid. Usually the target would come back at him with some line like, "Oh, really? My uncle's stationed down there! What company did you say you were in?" Flanagan would flame out and go into a flat spin and we'd laugh till we couldn't breathe.

The traffic in and around Annapolis on Sunday evenings moves at what could be best described as a snail's pace. This presents a major logistical hurdle for the Best and Brightest as they attempt to avoid being late for evening formation at 1900 hours. One Sunday evening at about 1835 hours at a bar in Georgetown, I happened to casually mention to my roistering mates that if we didn't get our keisters back to the Yard pretty quickly, we'd be keelhauled—if we were lucky. We had twenty-five minutes to make what is normally a twenty-five to thirty-minute drive along Highway 50—a congested thoroughfare—and get back in time to change into our dress uniforms before formation. After several expletives and much scrambling about, we hit the door at a dead run.

Being the Best, the Brightest, and the Most Desperate, we hit upon the brilliant idea of saving some time by changing clothes en route. Did I mention we were in a Jeep? With no top. On Highway 50. On Sunday evening. Driving like seminude maniacs. In the early twilight. Shirttails flapped in the breeze and BVDs shone through the gloaming as we slalomed along Highway 50 to the accompaniment of honks and jeers from our fellow motorists. Our driver was, of course, also trying to change, which was no small impediment to his vehicular finesse. There were several carloads of young women who gave us some vocal encouragement, but we never even looked. Is that devotion to duty, or what?

Have you ever tried to tie a tie while standing in a wind tunnel? Have you ever tried to put on trousers while trying to avoid a head-on collision at 60 miles per hour? Take Superman, put him in a phone booth with two or three other guys, and then launch the phone booth down Main Street in Metropolis, and you have some idea of what we faced. I remember thinking that night there must be a God because we didn't die on the chase back up Highway 50. I'm not sure whose pants I wore to formation that night, but I felt I had just survived a test worthy of Chuck Yeager and Mario Andretti combined.

I have to say that deep inside, I felt bad about the drinking and partying. The behavior seemed acceptable because everybody else was doing it, but I never got over the feeling that I ought to be doing something else. I wanted to stop, but I didn't know how. I still thought that by observing the savvy operators, I might begin to learn their tricks and maybe learn how to be "normal."

I became skilled at bar talk. With just the right number of drinks under my belt, I could slide into a conversation with a girl as smoothly as silk on bare skin. Before long, I was coming back to the Yard with dozens of names and phone numbers. Naturally, my friends assumed that I was the scoring leader for the Brigade—and I didn't do anything to correct their false impressions. Maybe if I could be perceived as a ladies' man, I could become one.

It was a lie—all of it. I wasn't getting close to girls, not in any way that mattered. I could still sense my anxieties simmering just below the surface. The partying and playing around were leading nowhere. The same blind alley was staring me in the face, and my old enemy was still inside my head, whispering reassurances of my inadequacies. The emptiness wasn't going away.

Despite the ineffectiveness of my Party Boy persona, it developed a momentum that became more and more difficult to resist. I was becoming a Navy man—but not in the way the Academy catalog describes. Besides, the whole culture of brigade life became a sort of gravity field. If you were in, you partied.

Frequently, the firsties would come in from their club binges during the week and brag about their exploits. "Oh, man, did I get totalled last night! Me and Kozinsky went out after tables and hit every joint on M Street ..." They'd laugh and talk about how plastered they were, how many women they hit on, how many times the other guy puked—all the interesting details.

And then, you had to up the ante. "Oh, yeah? You should have seen us last weekend ..." Of course, the firsties had an unfair advantage. They could get liberty any night of the week. They had more than twice the opportunities to indulge in revelry and maintain the midshipmen's mystique. As youngsters, we had to get it all done on Friday, Saturday, and Sunday—after church, of course. But we did our very best to uphold the honor of our class.

There was Palombo, the firstie who, for whatever obscure reason, "adopted" Brian Pirko and me. Palombo especially liked to come to our room after he had been deep in his cups, to share his blurred insights into the secrets of the cosmos. I mean, this guy would stay in our room until all hours of the night. Eventually, we'd get brave enough to ask him to leave. "Okay," he'd say, "but I got one more thing for you." He would then execute a somewhat tipsy facing movement and ceremoniously hawk and spit on our mirror. "Someday, when you guys are firsties," he would pronounce sagely in parting, "you'll find some youngsters you like and spit on their mirrors, too." We never identified the source or significance of this quaint Navy tradition.

As you might imagine, my academic performance waned during this period. I tried not to let it bother me. After all, I was maintaining passing grades. I wasn't in imminent danger of flunking out of the Academy. Graduation was the thing. If you graduated—even with a nominal GPA—you were on your way up Jacob's Ladder. The idea was to get by, to squeak through and have a good time while doing it. Lots of the guys used to bemoan the fact that by attending the Academy, with its strict rules and conduct codes, we were missing out on the typical college experience. This seemed to justify making up for it on the weekends and at every other opportunity. In the meantime, you rated what you skated.

But you had to watch the thickness of the ice. Some guys skated where it was too thin and went down. Conduct violations could get you, but honor violations were the kiss of death.

There was one guy who was separated from the Academy because he fibbed to another mid's girlfriend about his whereabouts so he could take her out on a date. There was a classmate of mine who missed a class because he overslept. A week or so later, the professor asked him his whereabouts during the previous session. He'd actually forgotten why he missed, so he just said something like, "I believe I was ill that day." They checked up on him and found out he hadn't been in sick bay, so they chucked him out on an honor violation. I knew of another case where a midshipman got canned just for cutting in line. What do these situations have to do with honor, with fitness to serve as a Naval officer? These are nineteen- and twenty-year-old people doing things that would be regarded as innocent pranks or simple screwups, at worst. And for this their hopes and dreams are torpedoed?

Instances like these were all too common, and caused us to fear the Honor Concept rather than respect it. Then there were guys like our company officer, Lieutenant Braswell, who seemed to take perverse pleasure in causing mids to twist slowly in the wind.

The company officer is supposed to be a mentor, a "sea daddy." He's supposed to help you learn the ropes, give you the benefit of his savvy and wisdom. But, Braswell . . . He would search diligently for some reason to accuse us. He'd harass, badger, and otherwise provoke us—always looking for any way to hang something on us. It seemed that his main joy in life was "frying"—placing on restriction—as many mids as possible. Braswell would make Captain Bligh look like Mary Poppins!

As if all this weren't bad enough, there were the situations where the Honor Concept was abused to put you in a corner. One weekend, Brian Pirko and I went into town, downed a few drinks, then went back to the Yard for one of those meet-the-debutantes-from-town parties. We were having a good time, when who shows up but our company commander, Scott Switzer. We're underage, and we know that if he suspects us of drinking, we'll probably get fried. And that's if we get off easy.

Commander Switzer walks up to us. He's all smiles and so are we. "Hey, Gantar! Pirko! How you guys doin'?"

Brian and I are busting a gut, trying to look at ease. "Great, Sir! Good party, huh?" We're laying it on thick, and Switzer is buying it all the way. We talk for a couple of minutes, and he walks off. Brian and I nearly pass out with relief.

A few days later, some firstie swaggers into our room and starts bragging about his exploits. Knowing that the appropriate and expected response is to come back with a story of our own, we start yakking him up about the party we were at, about how we thought we were dead when we saw Switzer, about how incredibly smooth we were in skating past him.

Lo and behold . . . A few days later, Switzer sees us and asks offhandedly if we had been drinking at the party the other night.

This is the classic no-win situation. We already told the firstie we were drinking. If we lie, we're guilty of an honor violation. (Mr. Socrates, would you prefer to fall on a sword or take a swig of this hemlock here?)

The *Honor Officer's Handbook* states that a midshipman's honor may not be used against him. His honor is considered to have been used against a midshipman when "(a) there was no reasonable cause to believe the midshipman being questioned had committed or was involved in a conduct violation pursuant to which the question was being asked, and; (b) the midshipman's answers to the questions resulted in disciplinary action being taken against him, and; (c) the answers provided were the sole basis for determination of guilt as to the alleged violations."

Just in case a smart mid might consider invoking this section of the handbook to keep his butt out of a sling, there's a note tacked onto the end of the paragraph. "Not answering a question because you feel it may be being used against you is *never an option*" (emphasis added). Answer first, then object if you feel that your honor has been used against you." In other words, give them what they want. You can legally object to the use of the coerced information, but when somebody calls the tune, you'd better sing—loud and clear.

We sang. We told Switzer that, yes, we had, in fact, been drinking before the party. To no one's surprise, we were brought up on conduct charges.

To his credit, Commander Switzer testified at our hearing that Brian and I did not appear to him to be under the influence of alcohol. We did not, in his opinion, smell of alcohol, nor act in any way that would have made him suspect we had been drinking. In other words, he had no probable cause to ask us whether we were drinking. The only proof he had was our own admission, obtained under the compulsion of the Honor Concept.

Like a good midshipman, I objected to having my honor used against me. The presiding officer for the hearing, Lieutenant Commander Rondeau, said, "Well, Mister Gantar, you were drinking, weren't you?"

"Yes, ma'am."

"All right, then. The violation stands. Thirty days' restriction."

He rateth not, neither shall he skate. Brethren, here endeth the lesson.

Eventually, such experiences tended to cause many of us to adopt a pretty utilitarian attitude toward truth. "Good" is what keeps you out of trouble. "Bad" is when you get caught.

In all fairness, I have to say that my youngster year was something more than one long slide into moral depravity. Things happened during that time that I am very proud and gratified to remember.

I suppose the biggest distinction that year was when our company was named Color Company. The competition for Color Company permeates every facet of Academy life: academics, extracurricular activities, military conduct and achievement, intramural contests and participation in intercollegiate sports. Points are awarded in every area, and a dedicated, concentrated, year-long effort is required to beat out the other highly motivated, intensely competitive companies gunning for the honor. But we did it that year. What a feeling!

At the Graduation Parade, the day before the actual commencement, all the companies assemble on the parade ground. Even the most unpatriotic person in the land would get chillbumps at the Graduation Parade. The band is showering the field with marches like "Under the Double Eagle," "National Emblem," and, of course, "The Stars and Stripes Forever." The entire Brigade of Midshipmen is turned out in parade dress uniform, spit-and-polished to the height of perfection, marching in lockstepping ranks as straight and clean as a plumb line. Thousands of people watch as the Brigade passes in review.

The reviewing stand has more brass than Ace Hardware—the Chief of Naval Operations, the Secretary of the Navy, maybe a couple of Chiefs of Staff thrown in. The heaviest of the heavyweights turn out for the Graduation Parade at Annapolis. And then, in front of God and all those admirals and thousands of taxpayers, they call out the Color Company for special recognition.

We had busted our humps all year long for this moment. As the band blazed away at a Sousa march, we moved forward, our special gold flag unfurling in the sunlight. You couldn't have moved a single pair of eyes out of the boat, not for any amount of money. If Sharon Stone had been doing a can-can in a string bikini on the sidelines, I don't think I'd have looked. We moved in unison, like a divinely anointed military machine, as we took our position in front of the entire brigade and received our honor.

There was cannon fire. There was a flyover by the Blue Angels. If you could stand in the middle of all that red-blooded, honest-to-goodness martial splendor, if you could be a part of it and not feel a catch in your throat, you were dead or worthless or both.

And the thing that iced it was knowing that, in twenty-four hours, I would be a midshipman second class. Despite everything, I was still on my way up the ladder. That, after all, was the bottom line.

☆ 6 ☆

DOUBLE-E

November – December 1992

IT'S SUNDAY NIGHT, IT'S 11:40, and I'm scared.

We're at Gator's, a local watering hole, and the firsties and civilians I'm with are polluted beyond all repair, and we'll play Billy Hell getting back to our quarters in time for Taps at 2400 hours. I'm not even supposed to be here, but what was I supposed to do—insult the firsties who invited me out? "Sorry, guys, I'm not allowed . . ." Yeah, right. I'm a young warrior, one of the Best and Brightest. I'm supposed to raise a little Cain every once in a while.

But if the duty officer checks my room and I'm not there, that's it. Unauthorized absence is a battalion-level conduct violation; it goes straight over the head of my company officer. It's precisely the sort of attention you don't want.

I'm looking at my watch and trying to get these guys out the door. Eventually, the shrinking time window seeps through their alcohol-induced fog and they decide to leave. Trying to decide who should drive is like choosing the ugliest pig in the mudhole. I know

I'm more sober than they are, but I'm just a second-class. There's no way they'll let me drive.

We stagger outside and begin piling into Wilson's car. She's giggling and squealing, trying to remember how to climb under the steering wheel, and it takes her at least three tries to hit the ignition slot with the key. And the clock is ticking.

She finally gets the car started, but her clutching reflex is impaired. The car crow-hops away from the curb and stalls. This is the cause of much jollity among my friends, and they strike up the chorus of "Joy to the World"—the Three Dog Night version, not Handel's. I'm wishing I didn't care about the fact that I'm about to be killed by Wilson's offensive driving.

"Hey, Wilson, hold it! I'm getting out!"

"Aw, Gantar, you pansy! 'Fraid to ride with us, huh?"

My options are severely limited at this point. I'd offer to drive, but her car has a standard transmission, and I've never learned to drive a stick shift. I can either get a cab back to the Yard, or take my chances in the Deathmobile. I get out and close the door. "You guys go on. I'll see you back at Mother B." As they weave into the darkness, I hear them jeering at me.

In the cab, I realize there's no way I can make it back in time. I'm going to be on report, called in to Battalion, probably drawn and quartered.

The transit from Gate 1 to the sixth wing of Bancroft Hall between 2350 and 2400 hours has become known as the "Gantar/Pirko 100-yard Dash." Brian and I have clocked some pretty good times on this track, but I'm afraid tonight I won't place or show, much less win. The cabbie lets me out in front of the gate and I sprint to Bancroft Hall and into my room . . .

. . . thirty minutes late. Brian, with a sick look on his face, tells me I have to report to the company CDO—the command duty officer. He will not be happy to see me.

After our little conversation, I realize it's even worse than that. He has told me I have to report immediately to the CDO for the whole Academy. Evidently, they're going to ask for the death penalty. I feel like a suckling pig just before a luau. I can already taste the apple in my mouth.

The Academy CDO chews on me for awhile, than drags out the infamous Form 2—the death warrant. Now I can hear the drumbeats and the sounds of the natives chanting. I'm fried for sure. It's just a question of how long and by whom.

At 0800 the next morning, the Form 2 is lying on the desk of my company officer—Lieutenant Commander Braswell. Up until this point, he had kind of liked me. All that is now in the past. I get thirty-six days restriction. Since this is mid November, that means I will not be able to leave the Yard for Thanksgiving. I had planned to spend Thanksgiving with Grandpa. It also means I will not be able to go home for Christmas. My plans will have to change radically. And my family will have to find out why.

I could tell from their letters and phone calls that my folks were starting to worry about me. Evidently, they could tell all was not well in Jeffyland. In retrospect, I suppose it didn't take a von Braun to figure out something had changed the outlook and attitude of the highly motivated, rigidly self-disciplined overachiever they had put on the plane two years before in Spokane. The kid who cried over missing a smiley-face sticker, the kid who got to school an hour and a half before classes to practice batting would never permit himself to get mixed up with a boozing, corner-cutting, rating-and-skating crowd like the one with which I was now involved.

I had to call my grandfather and explain to him why I wouldn't be able to use the airplane tickets he had bought for me to come to his home for Thanksgiving. Naturally, they were nonrefundable. He wanted to know what was wrong, why I couldn't come for the holiday. "Grandpa, I—I'm on restriction."

"Jeff, what are you talking about? Restriction for what?"

"I had an Unauthorized Absence." I wanted to die. I was admitting a major conduct violation to my grandpa, my idol.

"Jeff, I . . . I don't know what to say, I—I'm very disappointed."

The words felt like ten-penny nails pounded into my heart. And then, I had to call Mom and Dad and let them know they wouldn't need to hang my stocking on the hearth this year. It was bad enough only getting to see them twice a year—now that was gone, too. I could sense the anger in my dad's voice, the frustration and confusion. And I knew that I, and I alone, was to blame.

It was the lowest point of my life. I had tried to be the best, and that didn't make the bad feelings go away. Then I tried to outskate and out- "normal" everybody else, and that didn't work, either. I was on restriction for a major conduct offense that would be in my military record for the rest of my life, I still had the emptiness gnawing away at my insides, and to top it all off, I was now on Braswell's latrine list.

Braswell had this theory about people who had conduct violations. He believed that when you got in trouble it was like a snowball rolling downhill: lots of things start to stick to it, and it just gets bigger and bigger, harder and harder to manage. Eventually, it slams into something and self-destructs.

In retrospect, I suppose Braswell considered himself a conscientious officer who was trying to ensure that only the best, only the most dedicated and upright mids made it into the Navy. But to anyone who screwed up and drew his fire, it felt more like spite and vindictiveness. I knew I was rolling downhill, as far as he was concerned. I was marked.

Guys in the company would come up to me and commiserate. "Jeff, I heard you're on Brazz's 'special projects' list. I'm really sorry, man." Sometimes they would get word to me of things like surprise inspections, allowing me to be spic-and-span and avoid giving Brazz more ammo. They covered for me and helped me as much as they could without becoming objects of wrath themselves.

The one exception was Brian, my roommate. Brian openly stuck by me and took the consequences of harboring a pariah. I know it cost him a shot at making the Superintendent's List at least two times. He had top marks in academics, PEP, and conduct, but—I'm convinced—because he was my roommate, Brazz gave him B's in military performance, something almost unheard of for someone with Brian's record in other areas. In fact, Brian had received A's in military performance both years before he came under Braswell's supervision. In my mind, Brian's loyalty involved true courage. Like I said, you don't find many friends like that in a lifetime.

During these happy days, I got to know Midshipman Third Class Richard Wexler.

That wasn't his real name, of course. But let's call him Wexler, and I'll tell you a little story about what life in the Academy can do to certain people. The events really happened—I've got the scars to prove it. But let's change just this one name to protect ... everybody.

Wexler was in his youngster year, and he was getting his chops busted at every turn. He was on the football team, and, like several others in his position, academics didn't exactly come naturally to him. He was a good, hard-working kid, though, and he busted his tail trying to keep up. His biggest trouble started when he was accused by a professor of cheating on an exam. The allegation was later dropped—by everybody but Braswell.

Company Officer Braswell was on Wexler like a bloodhound on an escaped convict. He was convinced Richard was a cheater, and he seemed to consider it a point of honor to make his life at the Academy as miserable as possible. He'd hassle Wexler about his room, pick his uniform apart, rag on him if he was the last one to arrive for formation—anything he could find.

Life on restriction is about as serene and contemplative as Apache torture. First and most obviously, you can't leave the Yard for any reason. I suppose they might parole you for the death of an immediate family member, but I never saw it actually happen. On the weekends, when everyone else is at home with their families or in Annapolis or Baltimore or Georgetown getting plastered, you have to muster at 0645, 1015, 1345, 1515, 1900, and 2345. You have to report to the CDO in perfect uniform at each of these times, and he can—and often does—call a surprise muster at any time. If you don't get the message about the surprise muster and fail to show, it's an automatic Unauthorized Absence, and another 45 days' restriction. A real joyride.

Obviously, I wasn't hard to find during those days. Unless I was in class or drilling, I was never more than ten feet from my quarters. Wexler started coming around and talking to me about the hard time he was getting from Braswell. As I've said, Lieutenant Commander Braswell wasn't exactly a family friend at the time, so it was easy for me to lend a sympathetic ear to an underclassman who was also in difficult straits. "I'm tellin' you, Jeff, he's drivin' me crazy," he'd say. "He's even started askin' me about my quiz grades." Brazz had a sort of animal cunning when it came to harassment. He had picked up on Wexler's academic Achilles' heel, and he was applying maximum pressure. Wexler didn't need any distractions to hamper his academic performance, but Braswell made it a point to be in his face at every opportunity, dawn to dusk. To no one's surprise, Wexler's grades deteriorated to the point that he had to go to an Academic Board hearing. As a result, he was separated from the Academy, effective at the end of the Fall 1992 semester.

He had fallen off Jacob's Ladder. He wouldn't be entering the Holy of Holies. I talked to him about it some, and he made all the right noises. Told me he was talking to UCLA, that he had a good chance to play ball there and finish school. I told him I thought he shouldn't give up, that he should go on with his life, that he had a bright future, despite being separated from the Academy.

But he thought otherwise, evidently. A couple of days after his separation was announced, they found Richard Wexler in his quarters, hanging by his neck from the strap of his book bag. Apparently death was from strangulation, rather than a broken neck. It had taken him at least five or six minutes to die.

The suicide was a body blow to everyone at the Academy. I think even Braswell realized he had pushed too far. People outside my company were looking at us, wondering what in God's name was going on in 25th. All over the Yard, you could see shock and disbelief plainly displayed on everyone's face. But all that was just a bit late for Richard Wexler.

At first, I was angry—at Braswell, at Wexler, and at a system that could brutally snuff out all the hope of a strong, young man in the prime of life. I cried and I questioned and I sat in silence and stared out the window. I don't remember seeing anything in the newspapers about Richard's death. I'd heard stories about people jumping off the top of Mother B. or the Severn River Bridge during plebe summer, and I've since heard about a mid trying unsuccessfully to kill herself with a pair of scissors. But this was up close and personal.

Along about the time these events were transpiring, the Class of '94 was preparing for a thing we called the Double-E.

Electrical Engineering 311 is the most difficult course at the Naval Academy, but that's not the main problem. The biggest difficulty is that it's required, which makes it a pain in the shorts for every single mid at the Yard. The final for EE311—"Double-E," as it's called—has caused more ulcers and sleepless nights than any other exam. It's the one you dread from the time you hit the ground at Annapolis. Once you get past the Double-E, you've got it knocked.

As a systems engineering major, I was more prepared for the rigors of Double-E than many of the guys. The poli-sci majors, the history majors, the people who had never made the acquaintance of resistors and sinusoidal voltages and Thevenin-equivalent circuits—they were the ones who sweated buckets over Double-E. Remember, it's a required course. It doesn't matter if you're majoring in tiddlywinks. You still have to pass Electrical Engineering 311 to graduate from the Naval Academy, to get your entry ticket to the Most Holy Place.

On the night before exams, lots of mids go out and flip pennies at Tecumseh. The Tecumseh statue stands in a large open area in front of Bancroft Hall called Tecumseh Court. Tecumseh is standing, holding a bow and wearing a quiver on his back. The idea is to toss a penny into the opening of Tecumseh's quiver, which is about twenty or thirty feet off the ground. The opening isn't very big, and hitting it with a penny from ground level is pretty tough. So tough, in fact, that putting a penny in Tecumseh's quiver is considered most excellent karma. If you land a penny in the quiver on the night before an exam, you're considered to have all the luck you'll need in order to pass. Some mids would buy several rolls of pennies and flip them, one at a time, hoping for a miracle.

I flipped a couple of pennies at Tecumseh that night, more for the sake of tradition than fear of Double-E. I had more faith in preparation than in omens. Just as on many other nights, I didn't hit the quiver. No big deal.

If I had only known . . .

Brian Pirko, my roommate, and I were both pulling A's in Double-E and had been helping lots of other mids study and prepare for the final, but there were some guys who were in big trouble, and they knew it. One of the chief of these was Midshipman Second Class Christopher Rounds.

There were a few guys at the Academy who had come in from the enlisted ranks in the regular Navy or Marine Corps. Only eighty-five enlisted people per year are accepted. Most of the winners are credits to the enlisted ranks, and they make fine Naval officers. In fact, since they tend to be older and more experienced than the rest of their classmates, they often become leaders—either officially or unofficially.

But Rounds looked like trouble from Day One. This guy had been around the block lots of times, had all the street smarts in the world. Frankly, he intimidated me and lots of other guys in our class. I never was able to trust him.

Nor was I alone in my assessment. Chris Rounds had attracted all the wrong sort of attention during his entire tenure at Annapolis. During plebe year, he was one of the guys the upperclassmen were most determined to run off. The day we climbed Herndon, he had been up since dawn, getting hassled by the detailers. Lots of people didn't feel good about the prospect of seeing him with ensign's shoulder boards.

Rounds had over 200 demerits on his record. He was known to be a heavy drinker with frequent conduct violations. And he was about to enter my life in a way that would change it forever.

About a week before the Double-E exam, Rounds had mentioned to Brian that he was going to obtain some "really good gouge" and he wondered if Brian would help him with the solutions to the problems. Brian and I talked about it, and we weren't too sure what Chris meant. Rounds was supposedly in tight with a lot of the football players, and he usually seemed to be in on most of the best gouge. Everyone in our class was dreading the exam, of course, and Brian and I were helping a bunch of people who were borderline, so it wasn't as if Rounds' maneuvers were our main concern. Still, with Chris, it was always a good idea to nail down the details as much as possible. So, when I saw him a day or two later, I asked him what he was talking about when he said he was "getting some good gouge."

"Hey, Gantar, I didn't know you knew about that," he answered. "This stuff isn't free, you know," he continued. "Not for you." When I heard statements like that from him, I had the feeling something was up—something definitely not kosher. But it was the end of the term, and it was the Double-E, so I didn't cross-examine him.

Now, don't get me wrong. Neither I nor any other right-thinking midshipman at Annapolis has any problem with using good gouge. In fact, one of the main ways we helped each other survive academically was by passing around the most helpful gouge—especially football gouge. If, like Rounds, you had a friend on the football team, you were always trying to tap into the gouge pipeline. Gouge was like cookies from home—if you got it, you shared with your buddies.

So . . . Knowing what I knew about Chris Rounds, why would I go along? Why didn't Brian and I just tell him to get lost on the night of 13 December 1992 when he showed up at our room with photocopies of electrical engineering test questions?

As I mentioned, the Double-E is the most feared academic gauntlet on campus. There were people in our room that night who were afraid Double-E would knock them off the ladder. To have come this far, to have endured plebe year and all the rest of it, and to be eliminated because of a single course, a single exam—it was unthinkable. I mean, if you're studying English and your lifelong dream is on the line, how far would you go to get a passing grade on a test that had nothing to do with your major? Some guy brings you some test problems which he says will be really helpful on the final exam in a course where you're hanging by a thread. Are you going to quiz him about the source and purity of the material? Sure, we noticed the words "Final Exam" printed on the sheets Rounds brought us, but even that shouldn't necessarily have been a red flag. Copies of old exams were routinely passed out and pored over by mids, with Academy acceptance, if not approval. No one in our room that night gave it another thought. Gouge was gouge, and good gouge was better.

It was a little strange when Rounds started hitting up people in the room to pay him for the material he had brought. People who were really desperate sometimes did pay for high-quality gouge, but I never did—including that night. I think most of the people studying with us pretty much blew Chris off about the money. We worked on the problems he'd brought and mostly ignored everything else. It was about 2300 hours when Rounds brought us the exam copy, and we stayed up several hours after that, working the problems and helping people figure out the solutions to the equations. I'm not sure what time we went to bed—probably around 0300 or 0400. It was the night before Double-E. You could sleep some other time.

At 0745 the next morning a nervous group of midshipmen file into the classroom to take the final exam for Electrical Engineering 311. When everyone is seated, the instructor passes out to each student a ten-page sheaf of papers. When I receive my copy of the test, I nervously begin scribbling my identification in the blank provided on the bottom left corner of the cover sheet. "2/C Gantar," I scrawl, then "6522" in the section number blank below. After penciling in my instructor's name, I finger the sheets, waiting edgily for the prof to tell us to begin. He does, and the only sound in the room is the quick rustling of paper as everyone turns over the cover sheet to start working.

We have three hours to complete the exam. There are eleven problems, worth between eight and forty-four points each. Most of them are based on schematic drawings of various types of circuits and involve several steps and interdependent calculations. The first problem is a series of multiple-choice questions on descriptions of "ideal passive elements." As I begin reading the descriptions and marking my answers, I get the eerie sensation that I've seen these questions—these exact questions—somewhere before. A cannon goes off inside my head—Rounds! It was bum gouge! My face freezes with shock as I realize the "sample problems" we used in the room last night were actually photocopied from the final for EE311, Fall '92. Somehow, Chris Rounds got hold of the actual exam.

Even as I continue working the problems, part of me is locking up, going into shock. What to do? Should I get up and go to the instructor right now, tell him I can't continue with the exam, tell him why? And if I do, and people start asking questions, what happens to Brian, to all the other mids who were studying in our room last night?

More out of inertia than anything else, I keep working the problems. At this moment, the only thought on my mind is to turn in my paper and get out of here ASAP. Then I begin to rationalize. Maybe these aren't really the same problems. Maybe I'm imagining things. I'm tired, I'm on edge . . . Just keep working, and for heaven's

sake don't act like anything's wrong. Everything is fine. I'm working on an exam that was stolen and shown to me, and everything is
just hunky-dory. You betcha.

I resist the urge to look around at the other guys, to see if I'm
the only one who smells a rat. *Just keep working, Jeff, and don't look
at anybody. Get finished, get away, and then we'll sit down and sort
things out.*

I'm staring at Problem 7. "Vx is a 60Hz, 10V peak sinuoidal
voltage source . . ." I'm supposed to find the value of inductor L if
the power factor of the source is 0.6 lagging. I stare at the four possible answers, and try to remember if I saw them last night. Cut it
out! Just work the problem! You've got to show your work, pal!
That'd be a heckuva note—have the exam ahead of time and still
make an F. Rounds, you moron! Gantar, you sap!

By the time I finish the test, I feel as if the professor is staring
at me. I feel as if there's a neon sign hanging in the air over my head,
with the words "Dead Meat" flashing on and off in red. I can almost
imagine Braswell bursting into the room. "Gantar! Pirko! Pack your
bags! You boys are outta here!" I can't believe this is happening!

I get up and take my test to the professor's desk. Can he tell
something's wrong? Is he just waiting until I walk out, like the store
detective waits for a shoplifter to leave the store? I'm still asking
myself if I should say something to him. But he never looks at me,
and I lay the test on his desk like a letter of resignation. I walk out
of the classroom and I don't stop walking until I'm back in my room
at Mother B.

Dear God. What happens now? Everything flashed before my
eyes—my grandpa, my dad, my dreams of being in the Navy and at
the Academy. And then there was just the fear of wondering what
was going to happen next. *Dear God, how did I get into this mess?*

☆ 7 ☆

AFTERMATH

December 1992 – April 1993

B RIAN WALKED INTO THE room a few minutes later, his
face white as a sheet. We stared at each other, both afraid to
speak first. We knew.

It still seemed unreal. I never really thought anyone—not even
Rounds—would be able to steal the actual final exam for a course
at the Naval Academy. Oh, we'd heard rumors about stolen tests,
even about hook profs giving a few strong hints about test material
beforehand. But the whole test! It was almost beyond belief.

Brian and I found the problems from the night before. Looking
through them, we became more sure than ever we'd been parties to
a cheating incident of catastrophic proportions. "We've bought it,
man," I said to him, shaking my head in dismay. "There's no way
this is gonna stay under wraps. We're done."

"So ... What do we do now?" he asked. "Go back and confess?"

We found Rounds and buttonholed him. "Where did you get that stuff, man? This crap is gonna get us kicked out of here, you jerk!"

"Hey, you guys chill out! Don't get stupid on me! I'm not gonna tell you squat about where I got that stuff, and if you're smart, you don't wanna know. If everybody will just keep their mouths shut, everything will be cool, you hear what I'm sayin'?"

Brian and I went back to our quarters and thought about what was happening. Rounds seemed very calm about the whole thing. We thought he was crazy; there was no way under the sun for something like this to stay concealed. Maybe it would be best to just go to someone and tell them what we knew and let the chips fall where they might.

But, wait. This was Annapolis. For two and a half years we'd been earning a doctorate in Academy survival. This was the place where honesty was not always the best policy, where the raters skated, and the unlucky got fried. As we contemplated the probable outcomes of an admission of guilt, we remembered what happened with Commander Switzer and the conduct board hearing. When we told the truth then, we got pulverized—even though the book said we shouldn't have. In our experience, a person always got the death penalty, no matter what the offense. We'd seen guys get separated for things much less serious—at least by real-world standards—than possession of a stolen exam. The mere allegation of cheating—later dropped—was all it took to put Richard Wexler behind the eight ball, and the memory of his death was still painfully fresh. No, at this point, confession didn't look too appealing. The percentage in it was zero.

Then there was the question of bilging a classmate. We couldn't figure out any way to let anybody know about what happened without implicating Rounds. Chris wasn't exactly an Eagle Scout, but he was a classmate.

The only way you survive the purgatory of plebe summer was by absolute trust and reliance on your comrades. That's perhaps the main lesson of plebe year: don't bilge. If you sell out a classmate, you lose the solidarity of your only emotional and psychological support group. Rounds had gone through all—in some cases, more—of the disgusting and demeaning experiences that the upper-class dished out to us. He sweated out PEP, just like the rest of us. He braced against bulkheads and felt the stinking breath of some detailer in his face, just like the rest of us. He was with us when we climbed Herndon. The thought of ratting out a classmate—even someone with Rounds' obvious moral flaws—was instinctively repugnant. You don't bilge. Period.

And Rounds wasn't the only one to consider. If Brian and I started talking, how would we be able to protect anyone who was in our room the night before? These were guys who had no idea they were being invited to a Stolen Exam Party. They were, in most cases, just trying desperately to squeak past the Double-E. Why should they have to die for the sins of Christopher Rounds?

We looked at it from several different angles, applying all the wisdom we'd acquired at the Yard. And when we added it all up and totalled the score, it was Personal Survival 2, Honor Concept 0. As we saw it, the choice was between taking a bullet for an unrealistic—and largely ignored—code of ethics and living to fight another day. At this point, we were still on Jacob's Ladder. We couldn't see any benefit in jumping off voluntarily. We decided to keep our mouths shut and hope the whole thing would blow over.

With such cheerful considerations in mind, I watched as Brian packed his bags for Christmas vacation. I, of course, wasn't going anywhere, since I was still on restriction. I was at one of the lowest points in my life because it was finally becoming clear to my family and to everyone around me that everything wasn't okay, that I was not that gleaming success. I would go to the chapel between restriction musters and I would pray to the Lord for some road to take me out of my problems. But the problems seemed insurmountable and they were piling up on top of one another. I was in big trouble because of Double-E, I was in big trouble because I was on restriction, and I felt I was completely alone.

Before Brian hit the city limits on his way to the airport, someone sent an e-mail message to the electrical engineering instructor, warning of a possible compromise of the final exam for EE311. Pandora was out of the box, and all bets were off.

Apparently, quite a few more than just our little study group had a preview of the exam. As we later put the pieces together, Chris Rounds—and possibly one or two others—had scattered sunshine all over Mother B., including a couple of large doses in the football wing. Surprise, surprise, surprise. It appeared that the stolen test, or fragments thereof, had spread faster than the Asian flu. Scores of people were involved, and keeping it all quiet was like trying to carry water in a sieve.

Superintendent Lynch found out about the compromise the day after the exam, and he promptly called in the Naval Criminal Investigative Service, since it appeared theft of government property might have been involved. NCIS went to work immediately, interviewing anyone they could find who might be able to help them pick up the scent of the perpetrators.

As soon as the Brigade got back to the Yard after the Christmas break, late night meetings among small, very worried groups became common in the dorm rooms of Mother B. Guys would gather in someone's quarters to figure out what to do, what to say when NCIS called them in.

"What are we going to do, guys?" someone would ask. "I just can't get separated. My family'll disown me."

"After all we've been through—we gotta graduate. That's all there is to it. Craig, you're an honor rep," someone else would say. "What do you think—should we talk to Watson?" he would ask, referring to the first-class officer serving as company honor chairman.

"Forget it!" Craig would exclaim. "Watson's as big a fanatic as Braswell! No way he'd do anything but throw the book at us!" This was frequently true; the administration often promoted to positions of Brigade leadership the most gung-ho—in other words, the most rigid, unsympathetic, and self-righteous—firsties. Such types were usually referred to as "Honor Nazis." Their leadership was characterized by intimidation and the harshest possible application of conduct and honor principles.

Of course, for me there was no question of the result of any sort of disclosure. With Braswell already breathing down my neck, I'd be on the first plane back to Spokane. In our group, and for virtually everyone else, the pact of silence seemed the only way to insure continuance at the Academy. And that was how we played it for NCIS. We went in, took an oath, let them read us our rights, then solemnly assured them we knew nothing about any compromise of the final exam for EE311. "No, Sir, I didn't see anything that looked to me like the final exam." "No, Sir, I don't know anyone else who did." "No, Sir, I never heard anyone talking about it." When they got tired of our meek protestations of ignorance, they'd let us go.

And then, on 8 January 1993, they called in Midshipman Second Class Rodney Walker. Walker was a graduate of the Naval Academy Prep School and a good friend of Chris Rounds. The two had a lot in common: they were both smooth operators with lots of street savvy. They both thought the shortest distance between two points was an angle. And they both made me nervous. I'm not sure what was on Rodney Walker's mind when he walked into the room with the NCIS investigators, but my guess is he figured the best way to cover his rear guard was to give NCIS a sacrificial lamb—other than himself. Maybe one of the Honor Nazis had gotten to Walker; maybe he knew it was just a matter of time for him and thought cooperating with NCIS was the only way to save his skin. However it was, about five minutes after he sat down, the NCIS guys realized they'd hit serious paydirt. Walker blabbed like a DJ on speed.

According to Walker, Rounds had been bragging that he could get any final anybody wanted, including the Double-E. Walker denied requesting a copy from Rounds, even though Rounds supposedly asked him more than once if he wanted one. Walker told NCIS he had an "A" average in EE311 and didn't need an advance look at the final. The only thing he admitted to was taking money from several people for copies of the exam, and he justified that by saying he owed Rounds $100 and was trying to help him make some money. By his own admission, Walker collected $200 from other mids, which he allegedly passed on to Rounds.

Walker gave NCIS the names of twenty-five mids, in addition to mentioning the entire football team and two unnamed coconspirators. It was like he had the yearbook, going down the list in alphabetical order. I'll bet the NCIS stenographer developed carpal tunnel syndrome just trying to get it all down.

Whatever happened to "never bilge a classmate"? Rodney Walker didn't bilge a classmate. He bilged the entire Class of '94, and a couple of innocent pedestrians. He even referred to me as "Ganther" in his testimony. Such was the intimate nature of our relationship.

By 4 February 1993, NCIS had referred twenty-four cases of possible honor violations to the Academy Honor Staff—primarily mids who had either made admissions to NCIS or who had been implicated by Walker. The Honor Staff was made up of midshipmen first-class elected to serve as honor reps by their classmates. They would conduct the honor boards which would establish the guilt or innocence of the accused parties. Included in the initial roundup was Rodney Walker, Star Witness. Not included, for whatever reason, was Jeff Gantar or any of the people who were studying in my room on that fateful night.

As the honor boards began, a general feeling of malaise began to set in. Rumors were rampant of widespread lying and collusion among the accused and even some of the Honor Staff. One midshipman—later separated—testified that he knew some of the boards were rigged, that some panels were stacked with "cool" board members who could be depended on for a "no violation" vote—some of whom had been involved in the cheating themselves! Even worse, the flow of information between the investigating officers for each honor board was severely restricted.

For example, while it is common practice in such situations to "redact"—delete or edit out—portions of written testimony not considered relevant to a particular case, it soon became clear to the officers conducting the twenty-four honor boards that the cases were organically related. Despite this fact, the redacted reports received from the Academy administration often had one or two isolated sentences floating in a sea of white-out. It seemed obvious the cases were interconnected, but because of the administration's insistence on severely redacting the reports, many of the links couldn't be substantiated.

Some of the investigating officers found out that Lieutenant Commander Nagle and Lieutenant Cann, two of the officers appointed by Admiral Lynch to administer the investigative process, had constructed a matrix of possible associations between various mids and parts of the test. When the officers requested a copy of this document, they were denied.

Perhaps least comprehensible of all, the investigating officers were forbidden to confer among themselves to get a handle on the complexities of the entire affair. They were told the Superintendent didn't want "individual cases based on evidence concerning other midshipmen." Needless to say, this lack of coordination made the cases much more difficult to prosecute.

As if all this weren't bad enough, on 17 March 1993, Rodney Walker got up on his hind legs at his honor board and repudiated his testimony before NCIS, saying it was coerced and that he hadn't read it before signing. Of course, by this point, Rodney's credibility was on a par with the Hindenburg's safety record. I don't think anyone at the honor board was in much danger of confusing his oral testimony with the truth. In fact, several Honor Committee members objected to the highly dubious nature of Walker's statements at the boards and repeatedly raised this issue with the administration. At one honor board, the presiding officer asked for permission to show copies of Walker's original NCIS statement—which bore corrections in his handwriting—to prove that Walker was lying when he said he never read the sworn statement before signing it. Permission was denied. Additionally, witnesses who could have impeached Walker's oral testimony were never called. In the end, the honor boards dismissed nine cases against mids named by Walker in his NCIS statement—including Chris Rounds!—and found eleven midshipmen in violation of the Honor Concept. The frustrated Honor Staff, knowing they hadn't by any means accounted for the entire scope of the exam compromise, viewed the whole effort as an exercise in futility.

I wasn't exactly brokenhearted over the bungled investigation. At this point, I was still hoping against hope that I could avoid notice and keep my place on the ladder. There were about a hundred or so other mids in the same position, feeling the same way. If the story had ended with the initial twenty-four honor investigations, we'd have been as happy—and as silent—as clams. But things weren't destined to fall out that way.

The eleven "in-violation" findings returned by the Honor Boards were sent up to Academy administration for review. One of the eleven was Duncan "Duke" Ingraham, a star fullback.

Superintendent Lynch played football for Navy during the Staubach glory years, even serving as team captain for a period of time. No one at the Yard suffered more when Navy lost a game. I think he viewed each defeat as a personal affront, as if a losing season would somehow detract from his Officer Fitness Report. It would be quite safe to say the football team had no more enthusiastic cheerleader than Rear Admiral Lynch. But in addition to Roger

Staubach, Duke Ingraham's father was one of Lynch's teammates, and later served under him. The Ingrahams were, understandably, big supporters of Navy football, and Duke was a good friend of Lynch's son.

To the shock of the Honor Staff, Captain Padgett, the Commandant of Midshipmen, overturned the findings of Duke Ingraham's honor board, clearing him of any violation, along with three more of the eleven found in violation by the Honor Staff. The Commandant insisted he was not influenced by his knowledge of the relationship between Duke's father and Superintendent Lynch or that between Duke and Lynch's son. He stated he believed an NCIS agent's opinion of Duke's guilt, stated during the course of Ingraham's honor board, "unduly influenced the Board." About this time was when Duke acquired his new nickname: "Teflon."

By mid April, the seven remaining cases—none involving football players—were turned over to Admiral Lynch for final disposition. He expelled six of the seven, including Rodney Walker. And on the evening of 21 April 1993, he held a Superintendent's Call, attended by the entire Brigade, at which he intended to articulate the Ending of the Matter.

Alumni Hall sits on the west end of the Yard, across the street from Nimitz Library. Over four thousand apprehensive midshipmen crowded into the main auditorium that evening. Some of them knew very little about the Double-E affair, and some—like yours truly—knew far more than they wanted to know. No one knew what Admiral Lynch would say or disclose. But everyone was all ears as he took the rostrum.

He carefully summarized the entire affair, beginning with NCIS' best guess as to how the exam was compromised, followed by their investigation, the subsequent honor boards and the separation of the six midshipmen. And then, in a stunning display of empathy, he shared with us his glee that "no football players were involved."

The audience was instantly transformed into a mob in the making. A low, unruly rumble rippled around the room. Mids were staring at each other in disbelief, muttering things like, "Who does he think he's kidding?" And then, Rodney Walker, Erstwhile Star Witness, stood up and started yelling.

"Admiral Lynch, can you explain why Duke Ingraham came to your quarters the night before his honor board?"

It was as if someone had shouted "Heil, Hitler!" in a synagogue. Having gone through Plebe Summer and two additional years of ceaseless drilling in military discipline, the notion of a midshipman second-class interrogating a Rear Admiral was a fundamental impossibility—a thing that couldn't happen. And yet, here was Rodney Walker on his feet, pointing his finger at the Superintendent and grilling him like Lynch was some plebe who couldn't remember his rates. I noticed Walker was swaying slightly as he stood, and some of his words weren't coming out too clearly. That made a little more sense; a guy who had just been booted off Jacob's Ladder, who had fortified himself with about half a bottle of whiskey might just feel bullet-proof enough to do what Walker was doing. But still, the absolute insanity of the scene was mesmerizing—and scary.

"I don't recall seeing Midshipman Ingraham on the night you mentioned," Lynch replied, after a disbelieving pause. Now things were getting really weird. Rear Admiral Thomas Lynch was actually allowing himself to be questioned by an intoxicated midshipman he had just separated from the Academy!

"Then how come the next day Duke was telling everybody about talking to you?" Walker shot back, as the disbelieving murmur grew louder around him. The question hit home; not only had Duke discussed with a number of mids his visit to the Lynch home, he and one or two other football players had been bragging in bars that nobody could hang anything on them, that they weren't in any danger.

Admiral Lynch gripped the sides of the lectern as if he were squeezing Walker's neck. "If I did see Mister Ingraham that evening," he grated, his face purpling, "I don't recall saying anything more to him than 'hello.' Certainly, I never discussed anything of substance or anything relating to his honor board." By now, derisive hoots and catcalls were coming from the far corners of the auditorium. And Walker fired his next shot.

"Sir, I was approached and requested to wear a hidden microphone and record conversations with certain midshipmen, and you knew—"

"That's enough, Mister!" Lynch shouted. "You will sit down!"

And that's when the chant started: "Duke! Duke! Duke!" It sprang up toward the back of the hall and quickly ignited the entire crowd. I sat there in total shock, unable to believe what I was seeing: the Brigade of Midshipmen was committing open mockery of the Superintendent—a Rear Admiral, for crying out loud! It looked more like a street scene from the '68 Democratic Convention than a Superintendent's Call at the United States Naval Academy. I felt as if the Academy were teetering on the brink of anarchy.

One of the firsties sprang to the microphone and screamed at the Brigade, shamed them into settling down, reminded them that their behavior was not only dishonorable, it was disgraceful. Eventually, Admiral Lynch had to abandon his intention of wrapping up the Double-E scandal in a neat six-pack. He said he would allow the affair to remain open and that anyone with further information should come forward so their leads could be pursued.

He dismissed the Brigade, and we boiled out of Alumni Hall like a swarm of angry bees. If anybody had thought Admiral Lynch's little clambake would signal the conclusion of the Double-E affair, he now knew how wrong he was. The six expulsions were just the warm-up, and that was bad news for anyone who still had something to hide. And, boy, did I have something to hide.

CRISIS OF CHARACTER

Dr. Tom Patten

SEVERAL YEARS AGO, when Jeff Gantar was still in elementary school, I was stationed in Okinawa as head of the base Alcoholic Rehabilitation Service. I was a lieutenant at the time and had been in the Medical Service Corps four years. Prior to that, I was an enlisted corpsman and had served a four-year stint as a psychiatric technician. I was proud to be a naval officer and eager to tackle any assignment I was handed. I felt I had a great future in the Navy.

I derived a great deal of pride and personal satisfaction from my duties with Alcohol Rehab. I was good at my job and enjoyed the approval and acceptance of my peers and superiors. I expected nothing unusual when my commanding officer summoned me to his office one day to discuss an evaluation he wanted me to conduct.

My CO was a captain and a medical doctor. He was in command of the base hospital. He wanted me to perform an alcohol abuse evaluation of the command master chief, the senior petty officer in charge of all enlisted personnel at the hospital.

Immediately, I could see the potential for an interesting situation. It was well known that the command master chief was anything but a yes-man. He had been in the service longer than just about anyone on base—including the Old Man himself. He believed implicitly in going to bat for his people, and he didn't mind whose toes he stepped on. If he disagreed with a policy or a decision that affected the enlisted ranks, he would do so openly and without hesitation. In Captain's Mast hearings, for example, he would vigorously defend any of his people whom he thought were being treated unfairly. He consistently placed the welfare of his sailors above his personal popularity with the captain. As a result, he was highly respected—and justly feared—by the entire enlisted hospital corps, and not a few of the officers. Not to mention that he had occasionally been a significant burr under the captain's saddle.

The CO's voice oozed concern as he emphasized the importance of a thorough evaluation. "I want you to look very, very carefully and cover all the bases," he said. "This needs to be a very complete job." He spoke of his interest in the welfare of the command master chief and the need to get him any help he might need to deal with any drinking problem he might have. It was exactly what anyone would expect a compassionate physician to say.

Certainly, the CO's request was legitimate. As head of Alcohol Rehab, I had done a number of evaluations on officers and enlisted, from captains to seamen apprentices. I had recommended treatment for people above me in the chain of command, as well as some who were lower; the rank of the subject mattered not in the least. My only interest was in doing a professional job and being absolutely certain that any finding of alcohol abuse was backed by solid psychological and behavioral indicators. I was well aware that careers often hung in the balance, and I took my responsibility very seriously. If, for example, I found the command master chief showed signs of alcohol addiction, he would be removed from his billet and sent to treatment. He would be required to pass certain criteria before being allowed to resume regular duties, and the fact of his alcohol rehabilitation would remain in his service record forever. Not to mention that, if he really was alcoholic, I would be lengthening his life by getting him the help he needed; alcoholic chiefs rarely collected more than thirty-six pension checks. Of course I would do a complete job and cover all the bases. Why did the captain feel he had to emphasize that point with me? I left his office slightly puzzled, but determined to return with irrefutable results—whatever they might be.

As I was preparing to do the evaluation, a friend came to see me: a fellow officer. He sat down in my office and pointed at the file on the master chief. "When you gonna do that?" he asked.

"What are you talking about?"

"The alkie screening on the master chief."

I didn't know what to say. Technically, no one was supposed to know about the evaluation but the master chief, the referring commanding officer, and me. "Why do you ask?" I finally managed.

"Look, Tom. I know the skipper. In fact, everybody on the base knows he hates the master chief's guts."

I stared at him, not wanting to hear any more, but not able to stop him.

"All I'm saying," he explained, "is that it would be extremely disadvantageous, career-wise, to not give the CO what he wants."

"What do you think he wants?" I asked.

My friend just smiled and shook his head. "Tom, we're big boys. Don't be stupid, okay?" And with that, he got up and walked out.

I was stunned. I was being asked to commit a professional assassination on a chief petty officer whose only crime was standing up for what he thought was right. And my only alternative was career suicide. I was between the proverbial rock and a hard place.

Afterward, I caught myself hoping the master chief was alcoholic. If he was, I could make everyone happy. I could get him out of the captain's hair and help him get sober. Everybody could win.

But it wasn't to be that easy—if you could call that easy. When I did the screening, I realized there just wasn't conclusive evidence of addictive behavior. Oh, I could have stretched a point here, leaned a little heavily on an inference there. I could have made a case of sorts. It sometimes happened that way. I could have given the CO what he wanted. But then I'd have had to live with myself.

Several days later, I was back in the CO's office with my report in hand. I walked in and stood at attention until he motioned me toward one of the chairs in front of his desk. He was warm and friendly, asking after the health of my family and making the usual preliminary small talk. Eventually, he got around to asking me about the results of my evaluation of the command master chief.

"Well, Sir," I said, taking a deep breath and glancing down at the folder containing the report, "I did a complete workup. I checked everything there was to check and went over the results with a fine-tooth comb, and . . . I find no evidence for a diagnosis of alcohol dependence for the master chief."

"What?" The word was like the crack of a whip, hard astern from his manner only moments ago.

"No, Sir," I repeated, carefully placing the report in front of him. "It's all in here. I just can't see anything that leads me to believe he has a serious drinking problem."

The CO stared at me as if I'd just uttered blasphemy. "Well, Lieutenant," he said finally, "I hope you can live with yourself."

I felt the blood draining from my face. Mayday, mayday! Going down hard by the bow!

"I hope you can live with the fact that, because of your incompetence, a man who needs help won't be getting it."

I started to reply, but thought better of it. The captain stared angrily at the unopened folder for a few seconds and then, without looking up, snapped, "You are dismissed."

I walked out of his office feeling humiliated and angry. I had done my job! I had performed an excruciatingly thorough evaluation on the master chief, and triple-checked my results and conclusions. To get such an abrupt and hostile response from one who, a few days before, had seemed so solicitous of the master chief's well-being . . . I was enraged at the manipulation, the gross unfairness. An hour ago, I was a naval officer with a bright future. Now, I was wondering if I'd have a job in the morning!

Days and weeks passed, however, without any further repercussions to me from that uncomfortable interview with the CO. When I saw him on the compound, he was cordial and courteous, acting as if nothing out of the ordinary had happened between us. I assumed—or, at least, hoped—he had read my report, noted that I had done my homework, and accommodated himself to the facts of the situation.

In January, 1986, I received my FITREP—my Officer's Fitness Report. I was a bit disappointed to note I had scored in only the top five percent of my contemporaries. In order to be truly competitive for early promotion, I needed to be in the top one percent. Still, it wasn't a bad enough score to indicate a serious problem. I assumed I had plenty of time ahead of me to negotiate my way to the top of the heap.

In June, I was transferred to King's Bay, Georgia, where I reported for duty as psychologist for the submarine base. In September, 1988, I received a promotion to the rank of lieutenant commander. I was pleased with the advancement, even though it didn't come as early in my career as I might have hoped. I wasn't particularly disturbed by the timing since, at that time, a promotion freeze was in effect, and promotions were slow for everyone.

My next duty station was in Jacksonville, Florida, as Director of the Outpatient Mental Health Division for the naval air station. After about a year in Florida, I shipped overseas to become the Director of the Outpatient Treatment Program for the U.S. Naval Hospital in Naples, Italy.

I knew I would be coming into the zone for promotion within the next couple of years. I got along well with my CO, even discovered we had a common acquaintance in my old captain from Okinawa days. In fact, the captain was the immediate medical superior of my CO in Naples. Who knew? Maybe I had connections.

As a Medical Service Corps officer, my fitness reports and service record would be compared with that of five other officers at the hospital for purposes of evaluation for early promotion. I would need to stand out, to look really good in order to move up. The closer the proximity to senior ranks, the more competitive the process becomes. I had my heart set on making commander and I strongly believed my record and performance were good enough to get me there.

In April 1992, when the list of promotions was posted, I scanned the names, my heart pounding. Gradually, the adrenaline rush changed to a feeling of confusion, then disbelief. My name wasn't on the list! I'd been passed over! I must have scanned the entire roster five or six times, hoping desperately that I'd just missed it, that I would see "Patten, TG" somewhere . . . somewhere!

But, no. My name just wasn't there. Feeling crushed and bewildered, I went back and looked at my FITREP again. Yes, there was the one percent ranking, there were the A's on my criteria, just where I remembered. I looked at what the CO had written: "I most strongly recommend him for leadership assignments such as detailing and command billets, further training, and immediate promotion to commander." So . . . what could have gone wrong? Then I noticed where he had prioritized me for early promotion among the five administrators of equal rank at the hospital.

Third! Third out of five! I just couldn't understand it. For several days, I mulled and moped over the situation. Then I decided it was time to do something affirmative, to be proactive. I had to do better the next time. In about a year, I would get one more chance to move up in rank. If I didn't make commander on that attempt, I

Naval Academy dress parade where the midshipmen show their pride and discipline before a large crowd and a high-ranking reviewing party (left).

Graduation is the pinnacle of four years of blood, sweat, and tears. I could only watch this once-in-a-lifetime moment from a distance (below).

Age four, about the time of the abuse (upper left).

Jeffrey and Mark, ages three and eight, ready for a competitive and grueling game of football in the backyard (upper right).

The Gantars: Grandpa Mark and Grandma Margo, Mark (dad), Julie, Dorie, Mark, and me, all together to celebrate Christmas of 1984 in our home in Spokane (below).

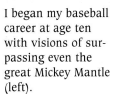

I began my baseball career at age ten with visions of surpassing even the great Mickey Mantle (left).

My dad coached my summer league baseball games for five summers before I started high school. This was my team in 1986 (below).

Navy football games are huge events. The Brigade of Midshipmen marches on to the field before every home game (right).

Plebe summer dress parades were a large part of a plebe's training (below).

The Academy grounds reflected my sense of loneliness and desolation as, during my third year, I spent the winter holidays on restriction (opposite page).

Dad and I doing some PT in the backyard only a few days before plebe summer began (right).

Grandpa Mark with me celebrating my high school graduation and my appointment to Annapolis (below).

Herndon Monument was covered in lard the day before I and my classmates climbed it and finished our plebe year (left). This day marks the greatest accomplishment in my life to this point.

Indoctrination Day. The plebes sit in Tecumseh Court and take their oath only minutes before F-14 Tomcats roar overhead, unnerving more than a few plebes (below).

'm heading toward
he on-deck circle to
ake some practice
swings during a
scrimmage at Bishop
Stadium (right). I
will always love
baseball!

Academy barbers put
he finishing touches
on the stylish hair-
cuts all plebes get
when they arrive
below).

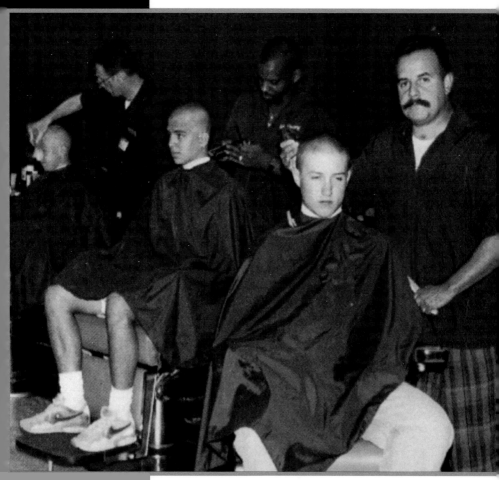

Plebes backed up against the wall, getting grilled by midshipmen second class (left).

A plebe reaches the top of the Herndon Monument, and victory is now imminent for the plebes as they begin to celebrate the end of their plebe year (below).

Brian Pirko and me after we finished the Marine Corps Marathon in Washington, D.C. (right). I met my goal of finishing in under four hours.

This is a Yard Patrol Craft (YP) like the one I was on during my first summer cruise up the east coast. That cruise gave me my first experience navigating a ship and getting seasick (below).

Angela Miller during her senior year at York College in York, PA (left).

Midshipman first class, Jeff Gantar, meeting Dad and Dorie after the Parents Weekend Dress Parade in September 1993 (below).

Academics at the Naval Academy are sometimes as demanding as plebe year, especially engineering courses (right).

Plebes try to concentrate on class. However, they can only think about what the upperclassmen have in store for them back at Bancroft Hall (below).

★ ★ ★

The EE311 involved most of the class of 1994 and therefore was an open "secret" among the members of the brigade. This sign appeared on Halloween 1993, mocking the administration's attempt to confine the scandal to a few midshipmen (left).

A laboratory from an EE311 class (below).

Midshipman first class, Jeffrey Gantar, a senior at the Naval Academy (right).

Here at Alumni Hall I witnessed Admiral Lynch being mocked by the Brigade, I was interrogated by the Naval Inspector General, and I confessed before the Allen Board (below).

★ ★ ★

The love of my life, Angela Gantar, on our wedding day, March 25, 1995 (left). That day, the sight of her stopped my heart more than once!

Angie and I in Baltimore in the summer of 1994 (below).

★ ★ ★

Angie's first visit to Washington state and the Cascade Mountains in July of 1994 (right). We came to check out the University of Washington and to appeal my initial denial of admission.

Midshipman first-class, Brian Pirko; Morley Safer; and me immediately after our taped interview with *60 Minutes* (below).

would be on a trajectory which would inevitably take me out of the Navy. I went to the CO and asked him what I could do to improve my competitive position for promotion.

He leaned back in his chair and scratched his face, peering at the ceiling. "Well, Tom, I don't know. I guess, if I were in your position and I really wanted that promotion, I'd do anything I could to look like a hustler, like a real team player." He reflected a few more moments, then looked at me. "Tell you what. I'm always needing more people to pull OOD. You might consider volunteering."

OOD—"Officer on Duty"—was an odious task, usually relegated to the most junior of officers. I had never in my life heard of anyone at my rank pulling OOD, much less volunteering to do so! It was a bit like asking A. J. Foyt to teach driver's education. Still, I felt my back was against the wall. This was no time to put my personal pride on my shirtsleeve. If the CO said pulling OOD would help me make commander, then OOD it was.

My peers couldn't believe what was happening. I remember the look on the face of the lieutenant at the desk when I picked up the duty roster and scribbled my name on one of the blank lines. "Uhh—Sir? May I help you?" he asked, his eyes flickering back and forth between me and the clipboard.

"This is the list for OOD, isn't it, Lieutenant?" I asked him, hoping I wasn't blushing enough to be noticed.

"Well, uh . . . Yes, Sir, but—"

"Thank you," I said, tossing the clipboard to the desk and walking away, my face burning with embarrassment. I remember thinking to myself, This had better work—quickly.

In addition to repaying the dues I had already paid as a junior officer, I needed to make myself as useful as possible to my CO. Surely, if I could prove to him that I could handle even the most difficult job he could dish out, he would see that I got the recognition I deserved. Before long, I had just the opportunity I'd been waiting for.

North of Naples, the hospital had a branch clinic, and the clinic had a serious systemic problem: some of the doctors there were having a major and ongoing confrontation with the director of the clinic, and the situation had deteriorated to the point that my CO had been charged by the naval inspector general to fix it . . . or else.

There were two psychiatrists at the command who were my superior officers. But guess who the CO tapped to do the conflict resolution? Lieutenant Commander Tom Patten. He charged me to go up there and bring order out of chaos, expressing his belief that I was the best person for the job. I was only too happy to oblige. I knew that if I could do a job normally assigned to someone of captain's rank, it had to help me in my bid for promotion. I told him I thought it would be a tough job. The battle lines had been drawn throughout the clinic, and everyone, officer and enlisted alike, had chosen sides. At least two of the combatants outranked me. I told the skipper that I had some ideas and would do my best. Then I said, "If I pull this off, I'll deserve a medal." He chuckled briefly and nodded.

I went to the clinic every week, and a couple of months later, the three warring parties were inviting each other to lunch. Surely, I thought, this would get the Old Man's attention. I had gotten his tail out of a crack with the IG, I had corrected the problem he had asked me to solve, and I had done it in record time. With cautious confidence, I awaited the approach of my next—and most critical—officer fitness report.

I asked the senior medical service corps officer to review my record and asked if my failure to be promoted made sense to him. He looked at everything and shook his head. I talked to psychologists who had been my supervisors and mentors during my career, and they expressed disbelief. One of them even said, "This is just one more thing that tells me something is wrong with this system." One senior psychologist who knew me only by my service record made the remark, "If Dr. Patten can't get promoted, we're all in trouble." Such comments may have salved my badly bruised ego, but I was still on the "down" escalator, as far as the Navy was concerned.

I called my detailer—a combination mentor and dispatcher—and asked if she could give me some idea why I hadn't been promoted. I was embarrassed to sound like a whiner, and I'd never spoken to the detailer before, but I was desperate to have some answers, some rationale as to why my career was being pulled out from under me. She, along with the others, expressed an inability to understand why I hadn't been advanced, but agreed to go over my records very carefully.

Eventually, she said the only thing she could find was a single FITREP from a number of years ago that wasn't in the first percentile. "But I can't believe that would be so crucial," she continued, "since it happened when you were still a wet-behind-the-ears lieutenant, back when you were stationed in Okinawa."

Let me add one important detail: Not long after being passed over for promotion, my CO had asked me to assume the duties as head of the mental health department for the hospital. I was only too glad to do so, knowing that my expanded responsibilities would bear favorably on my chances for making commander. I was actually supervising some officers who were senior to me. I thought I was in a very strong position.

In April, 1993, just before the ill-fated superintendent's call from several thousand miles away at the Naval Academy, I received notice that I had again been passed over for promotion. It was unbelievable, incomprehensible. After only twelve years as an officer, my Navy career was effectively over. It was now just a matter of transitioning out over a one- or two-year period. I thought of all the accomplishments I'd had in the Navy, all the achievements; I thought about being advanced to head of mental health for the Naples base. I pondered and I questioned and I sifted through my memories of my service history, looking for some clue, some hint of where I had erred, where I had made the wrong turn that sent me to this very premature dead end.

Okinawa ... I began to think about those days, about the CO's abusive reaction to my negative finding on the chief's alcohol abuse screening. And then I remembered that the same man who in a moment of anger had accused me of incompetence was the superior officer of my present CO. Not too long afterward, I learned that, even though I had been originally ranked second of five for early promotion on my FITREP, my commanding officer had sent a letter to my review board stating he had intended to place me third, that the second-place ranking was a mistake. And I began to feel angry and resentful.

In June, 1993, I received official notification that I would be required to retire from the Navy, effective 1 September, 1994. I had gone from being a conscientious and determined naval officer on my way up the career ladder to being a short-timer on my way out the door.

I was raised in a Christian home and I have always believed that God is in charge of events. Gradually, as the inevitability of the situation began to take precedence over its unfairness, I became calmer, more reflective. "Is this your idea, God?" I began to ask. "Is there something I'm not seeing, some reason beyond my understanding that causes this situation to make sense?" If, in fact, the five percent FITREP from Okinawa was what had held me back, if telling the truth about the chief's alcohol profile was what started me on the road to early retirement—would I go back and do anything differently? If I could make the decision again, what would I do? Evidently, I had crossed some sort of moral Rubicon that day, back in 1985 on the other side of the world. Without knowing it, I had passed an invisible boundary that would change my life forever. I came to the conclusion that I would do the right thing, the honest thing—no matter what. And if that meant a quick slide out of the Navy ... so be it.

As I pondered such thoughts and tried to imagine what life outside the Navy might be like, I got a call from a stateside Navy friend.

He wanted me to consider accepting a transfer for the last year or so of my Navy life. He wanted me to join the psychology faculty at the United States Naval Academy in Annapolis. He was the director of the Midshipmen's Counseling Center, but was in the process of stepping down. He strongly hinted he'd like nothing better than to see me take the director's slot, as well. Without knowing exactly why, I began to like the idea. In July, 1993, as Jeff Gantar was serving summer cruise duty before his final year at the Yard, I packed my bags and, with my wife and children, boarded an aircraft bound for the U.S.A.

☆ 9 ☆

INQUISITION

September 1993
Jeff

I APPROACHED THE YARD at the beginning of my first-class
year much as Marie Antoinette must have approached the guil-
lotine. Since the superintendent's call the previous April, the
Double-E situation had taken on the air of a full-fledged witch hunt.

The expulsion of the six original mids had been less like the
closing of a door than the tossing of a stone into a still pond. The
ripples just kept expanding and growing—finally splashing on the
shoes of some very important and persistent people in Washington,
D.C. The six mids felt they had been unfairly singled out, and who
could blame them? In addition to the noise they and their
families—in some cases, their attorneys—were making, all the
other midshipmen were outraged as well. Knowing how superficial
the initial investigation had been, mids persisted in writing letters
and leaking stories and generally not permitting the furor to die

down. Eventually, the noise penetrated the halls of Congress, and the secretary of the Navy instructed the CNO (chief of naval operations), in no uncertain terms, to finish what Superintendent Lynch had abortively begun. SECNAV referred the case to the office of the naval inspector-general.

Unlike the Naval Criminal Investigative Service, NIG wasn't charged with proving criminal activity. Their only aim was to determine who had violated the Honor Concept. Since no criminal activity was being alleged, trivialities like the Uniform Code of Military Justice and the Fifth Amendment to the U.S. Constitution went out the window—and with them, any concept of fair play. The NIG investigators subscribed to the medieval school of investigative arts. They would bully, intimidate, insult, or perpetrate any other form of mental and emotional anguish they thought might induce a confession. Anything short of thumb screws.

During the summer they had flown out to ships where mids were pulling cruise duty and grilled them for hours about the Double-E. Now it was September; all the little birds were coming back to roost, and NIG was waiting like Br'er Fox at the door of the henhouse.

Not that the mids had been idle all summer. Word of NIG's involvement traveled the grapevine at the speed of light, with the result that the guilty mids redoubled their efforts at weaving the best possible cover stories. Guys kept in almost constant contact, checking stories, manufacturing alibis, reassuring each other that no one was going to spill the beans. The paramount thing on everyone's mind seemed to be that we all covered for each other, that we hung tough, no matter what. As long as nobody talked, we thought, everything would work out, somehow. Double-E became like a sort of secret society; if you were a member, you wanted constant reassurance of the other members' commitment to silence. You frequently felt the implicit—sometimes explicit—pressure to go to the grave with what you knew. "Lie till you die" was the watchword, and graduation was the Promised Land.

Meanwhile, my personal problems were about to boil over. The pressure of maintaining a cool, collected façade—with all the anxieties and contradictions bouncing around in my head—was threatening to send me over the edge. I'm sure the crisis atmosphere surrounding Double-E was contributing to my instability. With the NIG hellhounds on my trail, I knew there was a real possibility I could wind up getting kicked out of the Academy. Separation, unlike my inner turmoil, would be impossible to mask. It would be a fact, an open proof that I was not, after all, everything people thought I was, that I wasn't good enough—or even good at all. I felt I was strapped to the nose cone of a rocket headed for nowhere. I felt trapped and helpless and scared and guilty. One minute I would tell myself the best thing to do was confess and get it over with, and the next I would be thinking about all the guys I might take down with me. Then I'd start pondering my old insecurities and rehashing all my old mistakes. I was a mess, and I felt completely powerless to do anything about it, except tough it out and maintain the classic Jeff Gantar front—as long as it would hold up.

I had survived my second-class year by the skin of my teeth. When I called home, my folks pleaded with me to please watch myself, to keep my nose clean. "Just hang in there for the rest of this year, Jeff," my dad begged. He swung between frustration with me for my bad conduct and anger at the Academy for what he viewed as excessively repressive, unrealistic expectations. "I can't believe they'd do that to a young man," he often said, "cause him to miss Christmas with his family . . ." And then, in the next breath, he warned me about the consequences of too much partying, of irresponsible behavior. "You know better than this, Jeff," he said. "You've just got to get your act together, son."

And somehow, by a combination of luck, the help of my classmates, and divine providence, I had stayed out of Braswell's way the rest of that year. He kept the pressure on me, but to no avail.

Eventually, for whatever reason, he turned his attention away from me and toward more promising victims.

But NIG could smell the blood in the water, and they were circling, circling, just probing for a weak link, for someone they could exploit to gain leverage on everyone else. I had made it past Brazz for now—but how long would I be able to avoid the notice of NIG?

Not that I was the only one having furtive thoughts about what might happen if I were separated. That dread hung like a dark cloud over my entire first-class year. It was the one thing anyone involved was most afraid of, but it was the last thing anyone mentioned. If we said it, it might happen. Every day when we woke up, we wondered if today would be the day NIG would call one of us in for questioning, and every night we breathed a sigh of relief that they'd missed us for another day. But, then . . . there was always tomorrow.

The one thing we hung our hopes on was the loyalty of our classmates. If nobody bilged, we thought we could squeak by. NIG might hammer on us, but if everyone stuck to the agreed-upon story, we didn't see how they could prove anything. The original NCIS investigations seemed to bear this out: only the guys who admitted cheating were separated. The guys who denied everything and stuck to their denials were retained.

NIG called in 673 mids, virtually everyone who had taken EE311. Their typical strategy was to show you a big stack of papers and tell you they had iron-clad evidence you were a cheater, that your best chance now was to just tell what you knew and hope for leniency. If you still insisted you were innocent, they would start yelling and threatening and insulting. They would call you every filthy name in the book—plebe summer all over again. They would find out personal information about you and try to manipulate your emotions. They brought in one female midshipman and showed her a picture of her boyfriend. They made cruel remarks about him, about their relationship, about what he would do when he found out about her cheating, her lack of character. It was prison-camp stuff. It was psychological warfare—and sometimes it worked.

Some people broke under the lash and admitted their involvement, even gave names of other people. Even though we had given our word to each other, some of the guys who were in our room that night mentioned my name and Brian's—enough times that NIG soon decided we were worthy of their concentrated attention.

Brian and I received our notices on the same day: "Report to Alumni Hall, Room 310, at 1400 hours, 10 September 1993." NIG. It was our turn.

Room 310 is very small; maybe twelve by fifteen feet. There is a table with three chairs, four beige walls, and nothing else. The room where Brian will be questioned looks much the same. I walk in and sit down and the two investigators stare at me for a while without saying anything. They ask me a few friendly openers about my family, my grandpa, my plans after graduation, and so forth. Then, as if by a silent signal, they switch to bad cop.

"Gantar, your friends have told us all about it, son," one of them assures me. "They told us how you gave them the exam, how you worked the problems—the whole bit. You might as well come clean, or we'll kick your butt out of the Yard."

No way! Those guys wouldn't just bilge me like that! "I, uh . . . I don't know what you're talking about, Sir."

One of them, a Marine Corps captain, picks up a folder full of papers and slams it down on the table with a noise like a gunshot. He leans over in my face and stabs the folder with a forefinger. "You're lying, boy! Every one of these statements says you had the test! And you're gonna sit there and tell me you don't know what I'm talking about?"

"Sir, I'd like to invoke the Fifth Amendment—"

"Fifth Amendment! Gantar, you don't get it, do you? This isn't some prissy-assed court of law, son! This isn't a criminal proceeding, there ain't no sweaty-palmed lawyer in here with you, and I'm giving you a direct order to answer my questions! Did you have the test for EE311?"

"Sir, I'm not going to answer, and I resent being talked to like—"

"You do? You resent the way I'm talking to you?" He sneers at me. "Do you know what my job was when I was here at the Academy, Gantar?"

"No, Sir, I guess not."

"I was a conduct officer. You know what that means?"

"Uh . . . Yeah, I think so."

"I used to fry slackers like you every day! I lived to get little cruds like you run out of this place! Does that worry you, Gantar?"

I shrug.

"Gantar, you're a disgrace to the uniform you're wearing! I'd like to rip that uniform off you right now!" He slams his hand on the table and heads for the door. "Talk to this punk," he flings over his shoulder to the other investigator. "I gotta get outta here; the sight of him is gonna make me puke." The door slams.

The other guy is a civilian, a former naval officer. He looks at me and shrugs, as if to apologize for the marine's behavior. "Jeff, I really hate to see you in this situation," he says, finally. "I'd like to do something to help you, but first you have to do something for me."

I look at him a long time, wondering where all this sudden sympathy is leading. "What's that, Sir?"

"You have to tell me what you know about the test, Jeff. It's the only way I can help you stay in the Academy."

I look at the top of the table. "I already told you, Sir. I don't know—"

"Don't give me any more of that crap!" shouts the good cop. "How'd you like us to call your grandfather in Florida and tell him what a no-good, lying cheater his grandson is?"

I can't believe this! Do these guys think I respect them, that I trust them?

"If you would just tell us what we need to know, we can help you stay out of more trouble," he says. "Your friends have told us what you did. You might as well do the same."

He's lying and asking me to bilge at the same time. I know that no one who admitted anything stayed out of trouble. And I still don't believe the other guys fingered me. As far as I'm concerned, the two NIG guys are the enemy, and I'm not about to tell them anything.

It goes on like that for about two hours; the same for Brian. By turns, they threaten and cajole; it's tag-team harassment. One minute they swear to alienate you from your family, the next they assure you of their concern for your well-being, your chance to graduate.

We come out of the interrogations exhausted, disgusted, and absolutely certain it won't be the last interview we'll have with NIG.

☆ 10 ☆

ANGIE

MY REBIRTH BEGAN ON October 20, 1993.

It was a Saturday, and I had drawn duty at company HQ. It was 2200, and most of my buddies were already gone from the Yard, well on their way to elevated blood alcohol levels. One of my buddies—call him "Garth"—came bouncing in. Garth also happened to be company commander. "Hey, man, let's go to Bohager's."

"Yeah, right. I've got duty, and my little can is staying right here. Brazz would just love it if I gave him another excuse to nail me."

"No, really, Jeff. Tex is gonna be here all night studying anyway. I'll get him to relieve you until taps"—0145 for firsties—"and as long as you don't leave your duty uncovered, you're fine. There's nothing Brazz can say."

Tex went for it, and I was sprung. Garth and I changed into civilian clothes and headed for Bohager's Bar and Grill. Bohager's is a favorite hangout for college-age and slightly older people looking for a good time. It's in a converted warehouse and has a huge dance floor and some of the best barbecued chicken wings anywhere. We arrived about 2300 and commenced reconnaissance on the large patio just inside the front gate. We talked to a few girls, but nothing was really clicking. About thirty minutes after midnight, I suggested to Garth that we go inside and see what was happening there.

Bohager's is always crowded, but on Saturday night it's jammed. We wedged ourselves through the doorway and stared around the densely populated bar. Garth was coming in behind me, saying something about getting another beer. And then I saw Angie.

She was seated at the bar, wearing faded blue jeans over a black bodysuit. She was with a friend, but I couldn't take my eyes off her. Garth nudged me. "Hey, Jeff, what are you doing? Are we going to the bar, or—what's wrong, man?"

I didn't answer. I just pointed.

Garth gave a low, admiring whistle. "Whoa, Jeff! You oughta be in F–16s, with vision like that, son! So, are you waiting for an engraved invitation, or what? Let's go, man!"

He shoved me toward them, into the swirling mob. I momentarily lost sight of her. When I saw her again, some guy was talking to her, but she didn't look too interested. When we were about ten feet away, we made eye contact for the first time. For a second, I couldn't breathe. Something about the way she looked at me made me nervous and intrigued me at the same time. I fought through the crowd and landed in front of her, having no idea what to say. I wanted to sound cool and controlled, but all that came out of my mouth was, "Hi."

Garth tripped and half-fell between us and engaged her friend in bar talk. Eventually, the old circuitry kicked in and I started my usual line of patter: "Yeah, I'm at Annapolis, I'm graduating in May, I'm going to request sea duty, blah, blah, blah . . ."

As I watched her watch me talk, I suddenly had the distinct impression that whatever I might be selling, she wasn't buying. She would make a polite answer now and then: "Oh, really? That's nice . . . Uh-huh . . ." I wasn't accustomed to this sort of nonchalance when

I went through my routine. She seemed to be monumentally under-whelmed by Jeff Gantar, Midshipman First-Class. She kept looking at me with an expression that seemed to ask, "Are you for real?"

I knew in my bones that Angie was different than anyone I had ever met. There was something indefinable about her, something deep and knowing. There was more behind those cornflower-blue eyes than the typical Annapolis groupie. I sensed she was a person of intelligence and discerning character. I was afraid to look at her for too long at a time, afraid she could see through my act and tell I was really a fake. There was no way I could maintain my facile pre-tensions of confidence and control. She was real. If I was going to be around her, I sensed I had to get real, too.

Garth and Meg, Angie's blonde friend, were getting along famously, I noticed. The four of us stood there and talked and time melted away. I was wishing I could stay there and talk with Angie for about ten more years when Garth said, "Hey, Jeff, it's 1:00. We'd better haul pretty soon."

"We don't have to go just yet. We'll be okay if we leave at 1:15, don't you think?"

He didn't argue; he was having a good time, too. And I think Angie liked the fact that we were taking a risk in staying a little longer to be with them. We strolled toward the courtyard, feeling the cool October air coming through the doorway. By now, Angie was starting to let down her guard a little. At the beginning, she was Fort Knox; by now she was more like Camp Latonka. We walked to Garth's Bronco and I was trying desperately to figure out how to see her again. In a minute, we noticed that Garth and Meg were locked up like Greco-Roman wrestlers. Angie seemed startled. I think she even said something like, "Meg! You barely met this guy!" Needless to say, I wasn't about to try anything on her—especially not me, and especially not then. Things were going so well, and I didn't want to do anything that might spoil it. I finally worked up my nerve enough to ask for her phone number, and—she gave it to me!

Yesssss! I grabbed the piece of paper like it was a hundred-dollar bill. And then I looked at my watch.

"Garth! It's 1:25!"

Garth disengaged and nearly yanked the driver's door off its hinges. "Oh man I'm sorry we gotta go I'll call you omigosh Jeff we're in trouble get in let's get going bye I'll call you okay? oh crap!" We squealed out of the parking lot and pointed the nose toward the Yard.

"Hell's bells, man! We're in trouble, but, oh, baby, we hit pay-dirt tonight!"

"Yeah, and if you don't step on it we won't see them again for forty-five days! We got twenty minutes before Taps!" The thought of being put on restriction—leaving aside the consequences for my military career—was like a knife in my chest. I absolutely had to see Angie again, and soon. "Go, man! Give it some gas!"

We were cruising down the expressway at about 100 mph. Garth had a radar detector, and I was holding it up at eye level in front of him so he could watch it without taking his eyes off the road. "Jeff, why didn't you tell me what time it was, man?"

"Hey, you were the one in deep liplock! What was I supposed to do, pry you and Meg apart with a crowbar?"

"We just gotta get back in time! I'm company commander, for God's sake! I can't get put on restriction!"

We pulled into the parking lot at the Yard at about 1:42. We sprinted to company HQ like our clothes were on fire, checking in at something like 1:44 and 59 seconds. Safe!

I went to bed that night, thinking about the piece of paper in my wallet, the paper with Angie's phone number.

Everyone knows that you don't call a girl the day after your first date. You wait a few days, maybe a couple of weeks. Above all, you don't want to appear anxious or too interested or, heaven forbid, overly committed. Everyone knows these things.

I called Angie at ten the next morning. The consequences didn't matter to me; I just had to hear her voice again. She answered, and we talked for about four hours. I proposed that she come to Annapolis the following Wednesday for dinner at one of my favorite places. She agreed, and I was half dizzy with joy and relief.

Even though she was from Baltimore, she was not too familiar with Annapolis or the area around the Yard—a fact unusual among young females in that part of the country, by the way. As I waited for her in front of the Academy, I began to question myself, to have doubts. Sure, I remembered her as incredibly good-looking, but it was in a bar, it was night, the lights were dim, I'd had a couple of beers ... What if nothing was like I remembered? What if our imagined rapport was only in my mind? What if I wasn't like she remembered? I had already staked so much on such a brief encounter. Was I building myself up for a major fall?

I saw her coming and stepped out to the edge of the curb, my heart in my throat. She pulled over and I hopped in the passenger side. I looked at her and all I could see were the two bluest eyes in the world. The inside of the car seemed to glow with the light from those eyes. Half afraid it was the wrong car, I said, "Hi ... Angie?"

"Hi, Jeff. Where should I park?" She was looking at me with a strange expression; I guess I was in sort of a daze—a combination of relief and disbelief in my own good fortune.

"Oh, uhhh—right over there," I pointed. She maneuvered down the street and into the visitor's parking lot. We got out and started walking downtown.

The Boardwalk in Annapolis overlooks Chesapeake Bay. It looks like a New England harbor town, with cobblestone walks, small, quaint shops, and lots of restaurants. We strolled to Griffin's and went inside.

Griffin's is candle-lit and intimate—at least at that time of day, before the Western-style bar gets crowded with noisy partyers. We talked, and the conversation seemed to flow more quickly, without the early hesitancy she had shown at Bohager's. For the first time in my life, I felt almost comfortable being alone with a girl! I kept thinking, I don't know if this is love, but there's something here, and I have to find out what it is. After a leisurely and thoroughly enjoyable meal, she walked with me back to the car and we said our goodbyes. I must have done something right, because I asked for another date and she said yes. Inside, I was high-fiving myself and rolling on the ground in delight, but outwardly I was somehow maintaining my composure.

As she drove me back to the gate, I felt mounting pressure to at least try to kiss her or something; it was, after all, the end of a perfect evening. She obviously enjoyed my company, and I felt I should let her know the feeling was very mutual. To my dismay, I felt shadows of my old, unreasoning panic looming in my mind. I leaned forward very slowly, then pecked her on the cheek and half bolted from the car. I remember the surprised look on her face. Later, I would find out she thought it was hilarious, maybe even sort of sweet, like a shy little boy afraid of his first kiss. If she'd only known.

We dated several times over the next week-and-a-half, and the more we were together, the more determined I became to find, once and for all, a solution to my anxiety problem with women. "This is a once-in-a-lifetime chance," I lectured myself. "Angie is like no one you've ever met, and you cannot blow it! You've got to figure out where these weird feelings are coming from and get rid of them!"

With fear and trembling, I began to hint around to Brian I might be needing some help, some advice about emotional and psychological stuff. This was as close as I'd ever come to telling anyone about my problem, and if Brian hadn't already proven, time and again, that he'd go to the wall for me, I couldn't have done even that much.

He told me I should go to the Midshipmen's Counseling Center. "I had some emotional problems, some family stuff that was bugging me, and the people there really helped me," he said. "They're professionals. They help people deal with this stuff all the time. You should go." At his urging, I decided to give it a shot. I was desperate. If there was any chance the Center had the answer to my problem, I had to find out.

☆   ☆   ☆

IT'S TUESDAY, 2 NOVEMBER 1993, and my guts are writhing like snakes. Today, I'm going to violate my lifelong defense mechanism: I will walk into the Midshipmen's Counseling Center and lay my soul on the table in front of a total stranger. The thought is like dipping my hand into a bowl of scorpions, but I'm willing to go through with it if there's the remotest possibility it can deliver me from my ghosts.

For as long as I can remember, I have been terrified of letting anyone know who I really am. The only way I have been able to cope with life is by keeping it at arms' length, by allowing others to see only what I wanted them to see. I had to run faster, jump higher, make better grades, and have higher goals than anyone else. It was the only way I knew to distract them from the shameful defects they would see if they looked at me closely. And above all, I could never let anyone know I had problems. Problems equal weakness. Problems are a sign of failure. And failure is the worst hell of all.

But the problems refuse to remain at bay. They're closing in on me, threatening to destroy my emerging relationship with Angie. The thought of losing her is even more frightening than making myself vulnerable to a counselor. And, after all, Brian says these people are professionals. Aren't psychologists ethically bound to confidentiality? It's not like I'd be telling someone I'd have to see in formation or anything.

I walk in the doors of the center, my heart thumping in doubletime. I can't seem to get enough air in my lungs and my palms feel greasy with sweat. I know my cheeks are probably beet-red; high color is a hereditary Gantar trait. I walk to the reception desk, my legs wobbling like a toddler on stilts. "I'd ... I'd like to speak to a counselor, please," I croak, my voice weakened by shame and embarrassment.

"Please sign in and have a seat," she replies in a courteous, efficient tone. "Someone will be with you shortly."

I scribble my name and slink over to a chair in the waiting room. My field of vision is restricted to my shoes, the floor. What if someone sees me? What if someone recognizes me—someone from 25th? I'm not sure if coming here is such a great idea, after all. Maybe I should just leave, before—

"Midshipman Gantar?"

There is a pair of shoes standing in front of me; women's shoes. The voice speaking to me is a woman's voice. Slowly, I raise my eyes to see a lieutenant watching me with a curious look on her face. "Midshipman Gantar?" she repeats, and I nod. "Please come this way," she says, stepping back and gesturing toward the door leading to her office.

I stand and walk into the hallway, feeling like a Death Row inmate on his way to an appointment with General Electric. She shows me into her office and I slide into a chair. She seats herself, and facing me, says, "Now, then. Is there something troubling you?"

The Moment of Truth. It's been a long time coming, and I find it's even harder than I expected. My throat refuses to form sounds; my mouth feels like the inside of a cotton gin. I look at her, then back down at my shoes. How can I say what I have to say—and to a woman! My fingers are clasped together in my lap, and I notice the little white crescents beneath my nails; I'm squeezing so hard the tendons in my forearms are starting to tremble.

"I'm twenty-one years old," I rasp, finally, "and I have never had sex with a girl. In fact—" Oh, dear God! How can I tell this? "—I . . . I don't think I *can* have sex."

A long, intensely uncomfortable silence follows. So long, in fact, that I raise my eyes to her face. She is watching me with a concerned, open look on her face. Finally, she says, "Okay, let's get some background information and then we will talk more about your difficulty." She looks over the paperwork I had filled out and asks me a few questions about family, relationships, school, and so forth. She seemed to sense my discomfort, because after a few minutes she asks, "Would you be more comfortable speaking to one of the male counselors?"

I shrug. At this point, my ego feels like freshly ground beef. What difference does it make?

"I'm going to make an appointment for you with one of our other counselors," she says, her voice sounding firm and decisive. "Why don't you come back on Friday? I'll have something set for you by then."

I may not have the guts to make myself come back on Friday. "Yes, ma'am. Thanks," I mumble as I stand and turn toward the door. I watch my shoes as they take the eight paces across the waiting room. Through the door and outside. Well, the cat's out of the bag. Wonder what happens next?

T o m: The lieutenant walked into my office, her brow furrowed. "Sir, I think you should take a look at this file. I think this client would do better with a male counselor."

"What's the problem?" I asked, taking the folder she offered and scanning the identification information, none of which meant anything to me at that point.

"He presents anxiety about sexual capability," she said. "He says he's a virgin, and questions his ability to perform sexual intercourse." She paused, and I looked up at her.

"I . . . I don't quite feel comfortable taking this on," she admitted. "I'd feel better if you worked with him. I told him to come back Friday."

I nodded, looking at the folder and thinking about what I'd heard. "I appreciate your concern, Lieutenant," I said. "I think you're right; this problem would be very difficult for a young man to discuss with a woman—even a professional counselor." *I really should take this case, but . . . My psych classes, the responsibilities of directing this center . . . And a young man in the prime of life, facing an intensely embarrassing and frustrating problem, a problem lying perilously close to the bedrock of his identity . . .*

"As it happens, Lieutenant, I have a good bit of background and experience with this sort of thing. Why don't you schedule Midshipman Gantar to see me on Friday? Say about—" I glance at my appointment calendar—"Fourteen-thirty? That should work."

She nodded gratefully. "I'll do that, Sir. Thanks for looking at this."

She walked out, and I looked at the folder for a few more minutes. Not enough here to draw any conclusions, of course. We'll see, come Friday. I put the folder aside and picked up the policy revision I had been working on.

Two days later, Midshipman First-Class Jeffrey Gantar presented at the clinic, on time and as directed. He was very neat in appearance: well-groomed, fit and confident. A bit anxious, too, perhaps, but that wasn't at all unusual, given the circumstances. I asked him to come into my office and we began talking.

His manner was cooperative and open; I detected no overt misdirection or hesitancy. His mood was neutral—neither excessively cheerful and upbeat nor morose and negative. I probed for any symptoms of depressive behavior or attitudes and found none. He answered my questions forthrightly and directly. I saw no evidence of disturbance of speech or thought processes. I had the sense that he wanted to be as helpful as possible.

He related a three-year history of secondary partial impotence; while kissing, he couldn't become sufficiently aroused, and because of this perceived failure, always abandoned attempts at further intimacy. He related an incident at age sixteen, which seemed to be the basis of his difficulty. He had not been able to become sufficiently aroused while kissing. He had had two or three beers—a lot for him—which probably inhibited his arousal responses. Whatever the reason, his failure to respond "normally" in this situation caused him intense shame and anxiety about his masculinity.

As he told me these things, I began to admire his determination and honesty. Midshipman Gantar seemed highly motivated. The very act of speaking openly about such extremely private matters is a hurdle over which many clients stumble. As any counselor knows, honesty and self-disclosure is a huge and all-important first step toward wholeness. Jeff Gantar seemed to be managing this stage quite well. I believed I would be able to help him learn to help himself. Because of his attitude, I thought the case was well in hand.

JEFF: By the time Angie and I had been dating for three weeks, I knew I was in love with her. Her birthday was November 13, and I wanted to do something really special to show her how I felt. I made reservations at the Chart House, a very upscale restaurant in Baltimore. I even had special menus printed that read "Happy Birthday, Angie!" I kept myself occupied with planning all the details for the evening, hoping the activity and anticipation would keep my mind off the fact that I was still lying to the whole world.

I thought going to the Counseling Center would cause my healing to begin immediately, but I was coming to realize I wasn't even being honest with the people who were trying to help me.

Dr. Patten was doing his best, talking to me about my sexual expectations, discussing various aspects of male sexuality, trying to desensitize me to my abnormal reactions to sexual situations. He was working hard to help me overcome the problem I'd admitted to him—my crippling anxiety around women. I could tell instinctively he was a caring, sincere person. I knew without a doubt he really wanted to help, and was thoroughly competent to do so.

But in my heart of hearts, I also knew I wasn't telling him the whole story. My problem didn't begin with the incident at age sixteen, and I knew it. There was something else, something hidden even farther back in the caves of my mind that was the real problem. I didn't know what it was, didn't know its name. But I knew I should at least try to talk about it—and I didn't. I was afraid to. It was the thing that constantly told me I would never measure up, that I was never going to be good enough. It was at the root of all my fears about myself. Somehow, in a way I didn't begin to understand, it was what caused me to flee intimacy. But it didn't have a name. It was just a dark nothing inside me, all the more terrifying because of its anonymity.

But today was Angie's birthday, and I was doing my best to shove such thoughts aside. I wanted to impress her, to win her. I wanted to show her that there was no length to which I wouldn't go to earn her admiration. I wanted to be good enough for her.

The evening was all I'd hoped. Angie was radiant, and every smile, every laugh went straight to my heart. She seemed to really enjoy my company, which was like medicine to my soul. The food, the atmosphere, the talk—everything was perfect.

And then, on the drive back to Angie's place, something happened. She reached over and affectionately stroked my leg. Nothing suggestive or lewd, even in the slightest. Just a familiar, loving touch. But that touch unleashed a raging demon inside my mind.

Angie could sense my agony. "Jeff, what's wrong?" she asked, her voice rising in alarm. "What happened?"

Somehow, I kept the car on the road until we got to her apartment. I stumbled through the living room and collapsed on her bed. "Jeff, you're scaring me! Tell me what—is—wrong!"

I hear her voice, but it seems far away. The walls of her room are fading, and I am falling through, going back, seeing it happen—living again the darkest, most shameful, most terrifying hour of my life. It is the year 1976, and I am four years old . . .

☆ 11 ☆
NAMING THE GHOST

MOMMY AND DADDY ARE *going out tonight. I know because they have changed clothes and Mommy smells nice. I like it when they go—I get to wrestle with my brother and get away with more stuff than when they're home. And I get to eat my favorite food for dinner: Chef Boy-ar-dee spaghetti and meatballs! I bet the babysitter will let me stay up later and watch TV, too.*

Mommy comes toward me. She has red lips. She kisses me and tells me to be a good boy. She walks past me toward the door. Daddy is there, looking at his watch and talking to a tall lady—the babysitter. She looks like the big school kids I sometimes see walking past our house on their way to the junior high, but still she is almost as tall as my daddy. She smiles at me. I like her.

Mark and I gobble up our spaghetti. After dinner, we sit down in front of the TV and the babysitter talks on the phone for awhile. She glances at me sometimes and smiles. I think she likes me, and that makes me feel good.

After a while, she comes over to where Mark and I are watching TV. She takes my hand. "Let's go upstairs for a minute," she says. I smile at her and go with her. Mark is watching one of his favorite shows, so he barely notices when I leave.

She goes up the stairs faster than I can go. Her fingers dig into my arm as she pulls me. Why is she in such a hurry all of a sudden? She is starting to hurt my arm, and I pull back a little, but she pulls me up the stairs anyway. I don't like the way she's treating me now. I'm not a baby! I can walk up the stairs by myself, but she is acting like she doesn't care. Why is she acting this way? I thought she liked me.

I wonder if she is going to play a game with me. That might be fun—just the babysitter and me! Mark wouldn't get to play, because the babysitter likes me more than him! Maybe she wants to show me a new game and that's why she's in such a hurry. But I still wish she wouldn't pinch my arm so much. It hurts.

We're going into the upstairs bathroom. She reaches around the corner of the doorway and switches on the light. The tub and toilet are bright white, and there is a big mirror on one wall. When we are inside, she closes the door and locks it. Oh, boy! It really is a secret game, and Mark can't play! I start to smile, wondering what we'll do next. This babysitter has lots of fun and surprises! She doesn't ignore me, like the other babysitters sometimes do. She thinks I'm special, and she wants to spend some time just with me.

She turns around and looks down at me. Her eyes are dark brown, not blue like mine. Her hair is brown, too. She seems even taller now, looking down at me. She looks at me for a long time, and I look back at her, smiling, ready to learn the new, secret, special game.

But she doesn't look happy now. Her face is serious, and she doesn't look like someone who is getting ready to play a game. Then she asks me a question.

"Jeffey, do you want to be a big boy?"

Easy! "Yeah, I sure do! I want to be big just like my daddy!" I'm starting to get a little confused; she looks so stern, and why would she ask me such a funny question?

She smiles at me, but it isn't a nice smile, like before. I don't like this smile, it makes me start to get nervous. I wish I was back with Mark, watching TV.

"Jeffey, do you want me to show you what big boys do?" she asks.

I'm embarrassed to answer, and I don't know what to say. I don't like the way she's talking to me now. I squirm and look around, trying not to look at her face.

"Jeffey, answer me! You won't ever know what big boys do unless I help you. Do you want me to help you?"

I'm starting to get a little bit scared, but if I don't answer her, I'm afraid she'll get really mad. "I—I guess so," I say, very softly. I still can't look at her. Then I hear a rustling sound, and I look up.

She is taking off her clothes! I can't believe it! This is a bad thing, and I know it. But she keeps on going, taking off her dress, then her underwear. She is naked, and she is still staring down at me with that mean look on her face. I don't know what to do. The bathroom isn't very big, and she is right in front of me. No matter what I do, I can't get away from her, away from the strange, scary sight of her body, her secret places. I stare at the pile of clothes, and I wish, I wish, I wish she'd put them on again and let me go downstairs. But she doesn't put them on.

"Now it's your turn, Jeffey."

I know what she means, but I can't do that! I can't take off my clothes in front of a stranger—a girl! "I don't want to," I say. My lips start to feel funny, and my throat is hurting, like right before I start crying.

She grabs me, and her fingernails dig into my shoulders. It hurts!

"Take your clothes off!" Her voice is mean, and I can see her teeth. Why is she mad at me? Did I do something wrong?

"No, I don't want to!"

Her face is right up against mine. I'm really scared. I can feel my eyes burning and feel the tears running down my face. She starts pulling out my shirttail and unbuttoning my pants. She's so much bigger and stronger than me, and I can't fight her. She yanks my shirt over my head and the buttons scratch my face. I'm too afraid to move. Why is this happening? Why is she being mean to me?

Her eyes are wide and staring—they don't look like a nice person's eyes anymore. She is like someone crazy, and she doesn't stop until she has taken off all my clothes and underwear. I am so ashamed, but I don't know what to do. She is bigger than me. I'm afraid she'll hurt me really bad if I don't do what she says.

When she has my clothes off, she stands up again and looks down at me, her hands on her hips. She picks me up and sets me down hard on the cold toilet seat. Then she grabs me—down there. She's touching me where no one but my parents is supposed to touch! Oh, please let her stop! Please, please, please make her stop!

She grabs my hand and makes me touch her. This is wrong, wrong, wrong! People aren't supposed to do this! Why is she doing these bad, ugly things, and why is she making me do them? I don't want to do these things, and they don't feel nice, and I know this is the most terrible thing that has ever happened to me. She's making scary sounds, like some kind of animal. Why won't she leave me alone? Please, God, make this stop, make this not happen! I feel tears running and running down my cheeks, but I'm too scared to make a sound. I'm afraid she'll hurt me even more.

"No!" I try to say, but my mouth won't make any noise. She is squeezing my hand so hard it's going numb. The nastiness seems to go on and on and on. I close my eyes, afraid to look at her anymore.

What did I do to make her so mad at me? What did I do that was so bad? She stops and looks at me. She seems even more angry now! "What's wrong with you? Why can't you be a big boy?" she says in a scolding voice. She hates me! I've done something wrong, something she didn't want me to do, but I don't know what. I can't understand why she is treating me this way.

A car pulls into the driveway of our house. She hears the sound, and quickly begins putting her clothes back on. She dresses herself, then puts my clothes back on me. She is very rough with me, shoving me back and forth as she dresses me, but I keep my eyes closed, afraid to look at anything, afraid I'll do something else that's wrong. Then she *grabs my shoulders again, digging her nails in. The pain makes me open my eyes, and her face is right in front of me again.*

"Don't you tell anyone what happened!" she says angrily. "You are a bad boy! If you tell, everyone will know you are a bad boy!" Then she shoves me out the door.

I hear Mommy and Daddy coming through the front door. I race down the stairs and grab Mommy's leg, hiding my face in her dress. I am so scared, I don't think I'll ever let go. "Help me, Mommy," I think, but I'm still too scared to talk. And then the babysitter is coming down the stairs, smiling at my parents!

The sound of her voice makes me afraid all over again. Even though she sounds nice now, I know she hates me. I know she thinks I'm a bad boy. The only thing that keeps me safe is Mommy, and I grip her leg even tighter. Make her go away, Daddy! She hurt me! But—no! If I tell . . .

She finally leaves our house, but deep inside, I still feel scared, still feel like a bad boy. Sometimes at night, I have scary dreams. I wake up alone and afraid, and I have to go climb in bed with Mommy and Daddy. If I hold onto them, maybe I'll be safe . . .

I'm holding onto Angie, and I'm sobbing in deep, wet gasps. As the horrible, hateful memory pours out of the hidden vault inside me, I feel once again as I felt all those years ago, gripping my mother's leg. I can't let go of Angie, because her nearness is the only thing that lets me feel safe.

Angie is crying, too, and gently stroking the back of my head. "Oh, Jeff! Jeff! What a horrible thing to do to an innocent child! Oh, dear Lord! Jeff, you poor thing . . ."

I'm a bad boy, a bad boy, a bad boy . . . Could it be that the ceaseless litany of my interior accuser was planted in me that night? Could that moment of shame, of burning, blinding terror have spawned my lifelong quest for acceptance and approval and, at the same time, insured I would never find either? A bad boy, a bad boy . . . Was that where the message came from?

"Jeff, you've got to talk to someone about this," Angie says. "You've got to get some professional help to deal with it. That girl did something unspeakable to you that night, and you've been carrying it around all these years. It's killing you, and you've got to get help."

She's right. I have to attack this problem, to name it out loud. No matter how painful it will be to relive those horrifying moments another time, I know I must.

"Is there anyone at the Academy you can talk to?" she asks. "Anyone you trust?"

Maybe. There just might be someone like that. I'll find out on Monday.

The next Monday afternoon I was seated in the waiting room at the Midshipmen's Counseling Center.

TOM: When Midshipman Gantar walked into my office, I sensed immediately that something in him had changed. He appeared both more nervous and more determined than usual, and from his facial expression and gestures I had the impression he was dreading what he would tell me, but absolutely insistent on seeing it through.

"What's up, Jeff?" I asked, as we sat down.

"Something happened to me this weekend," he began, his voice hesitant, his eyes avoiding mine. "I have to tell you about it."

"Have to tell me?" My instincts were telling me that something major was about to happen, and I strained to catch every nuance, every inflection, every gesture.

"Yeah, I don't really want to talk about it, but I think I have to get it out."

Careful, Tom. "Okay. Do you want to just tell me, or do you need a little help?"

His fingers twined nervously in his lap. "I think I can do it."

"Fine. Whenever you're ready."

He told me.

He told me what happened when Angie touched him, of his spontaneous, onrushing memory of the night when he was four years old. With tears gushing down his cheeks, he told the story in a quick voice, without looking at me, as though he were taking a dose of the worst medicine imaginable and wanted it over with as quickly as possible.

When he finished, neither of us spoke for some moments. He looked at me, and his reddened eyes were begging silently for help. I was at once enraged and heartbroken. Seldom have I been so overcome with the vastness of a client's need, or so conscious of my fearful responsibility as a counselor. I took a deep breath, said a quick, silent prayer, and stepped into the minefield.

"Jeff, do you want to ask me something?"

He told me later he felt like a huddled ball of shame. He looked at me, and with a wavering voice asked the question I knew he dreaded most of all. "Doc, what do you think of me now? Do you still like me?"

"Absolutely! I am amazed by your honesty and courage and I have more respect for you now than ever before."

I told him that he must completely believe me when I said the molestation was in no way his fault. That sounds ridiculous to someone who's never felt the shame, the shock, and the isolation brought on by such an incident, but I knew it was totally necessary to get Jeff to accept his blamelessness. Such acceptance was paramount to helping him begin resolving the emotional trauma he had suffered that night, so many years ago. When the molester said, "You're a bad boy," she had robbed him of his innocence. Somehow, Jeff had to recover it, to absolve himself of the lifelong, haunting, undeserved sense of guilt.

Jeff had revealed to me the name of the beast. Now I had to help him cast it into the abyss.

☆ 12 ☆

TRUTH
HEALS

EVEALING THE ABUSIVE INCIDENT to Dr. Patten was
like diving headfirst off a pier into a pond of unknown depth.
It went against every instinct I knew, and the thought of doing it
scared me to death. But, once it was done, once he assured me of
his continued acceptance and respect—respect!—it felt like coming up from fifty feet underwater and sucking in a lungful of air. I
had told another human being the worst, darkest, most shameful
secret I had, and he could look me in the eye and tell me I was still
okay, as far as he was concerned. And the way Dr. Patten looked and
sounded, it never occurred to me to doubt him.

It was as if I'd discovered a key that someone had hidden. Over
the course of the next few weeks, Doc began showing me how
understanding what had happened to me could unlock so many of
the problems I was having. Difficulty with women was pretty
obvious; when a girl touched me or got too close, my subconscious

was reacting the same way I had in that upstairs bathroom when I was four. The intense discomfort, the feelings of guilt and shame— it was all tied to that horrible night in my childhood. And as for the constant, nagging sense of being wrong, bad, not good enough, Doc helped me begin to see how the suppressed and misplaced feelings about the abuse had turned in on me, had created deep within me a constantly looping tape of accusations and threats and fear of openness.

It wasn't as though surfacing the suppressed memory instantly made everything okay, however. Doc had his work cut out for him in getting me to accept, to really accept, that I couldn't have done anything to deserve, prevent, or foster the abuse. He had to sell me hard on the fact that I was innocent, pure and simple.

"Jeff," Dr. Patten asked, "why didn't you yell for help?"

"I tried, but I was too scared. I couldn't."

"Why were you scared?"

"What was happening was wrong. I didn't know what to do. She was doing something to me that she was not supposed to."

"Jeff, what would have happened if you had yelled or hit her?"

"She would have been more angry with me. I wish I would have fought her more. I should have. . . . But she might have done something worse to me."

"So it was smarter of you not to have yelled or hit her. You were taking care of yourself the best you could. Jeff, is being afraid of someone bigger and stronger something for a little boy to be ashamed of?"

"No."

"So what do you have to be ashamed of?"

"It seems pretty stupid for me to blame myself, but that's the way I feel. You're right, there's nothing I could have done. She was twice as big as me. I shouldn't feel guilty about what happened, but I do. I don't have the problem, the babysitter is the one who is sick, not me. Right?"

"Absolutely. I understand that you still feel a little guilty, even though you know there is no reason for you to. As your understanding that you are not responsible for what happened grows stronger, you will feel less and less ashamed."

"I hope so."

I remember in one session, after he had once more presented all the emotional, logical, and therapeutic reasons I should let myself off the hook, he suddenly got out of his chair and stepped onto the small coffee table between the chairs. He stood right on the edge of the table, within inches of my knees, crossed his arms on his chest and scowled down at me with stern disapproval etched in his features.

I couldn't imagine what had suddenly transformed my trusted counselor and confidant into a domineering, scowling accuser. I felt the blood draining from my face. *Oh, man! I've done it, now! I've been stupid enough to get even Doc mad at me!*

"Are you going to tell me to get down?" he half yelled at me.

I stared up at him, unable to speak. All I could do was shake my head.

"Are you going to tell me not to do this?"

"I . . . I can't," I said in a choked voice.

He got down off the table, sat in his chair and leaned forward, his elbows on his knees. "Jeff, how did you feel, looking up at me and hearing what I said?" His voice was Doc's again, the friend, the one who wanted to help.

Confused and a little disoriented, I shrugged and searched for words. "Uhh, I was . . . I was pretty—intimidated, I guess."

"Jeff, listen to me! That babysitter looked even bigger and more powerful to that four-year-old than I looked to you, just now. How can you think that little boy was in any way responsible for what happened? How could he have exerted any control? How could any of it have been his fault?"

The light started to brighten. Or, maybe it would be better to say the sun started to rise. I felt my shoulders straightening, felt my chin coming up. It was like a religious awakening, like a sudden, unexpected experience of grace. It wasn't my fault! I'm not a bad boy! There's nothing wrong with me! I don't have to be ashamed anymore!

If Doctor Patten had never done anything for me other than lead me to the brink of that moment of deliverance, that alone would be enough to make me respect him until my dying day.

I began to see that honesty was the only path to healing, not only for my sexual problems, but also for my self-esteem difficulties—in short, for everything else wrong in my life. Dr. Patten knew this, and constantly pushed me to be honest with myself and with everyone else. But I couldn't instantly release my fear of self-revelation. I still couldn't believe that I could be truly honest about myself with anyone else and still keep their friendship or respect.

One day, Doc looked me in the eye and asked, "Jeff, what's the worst thing you've ever done?"

I felt my chest tightening. Could I really believe him? Could anyone know the truth about me and still maintain a relationship with me? "Well, I've committed an honor violation," I said, not quite believing the sound of my own voice.

I had just said the unthinkable, admitted the Original Sin of the Naval Academy. With great difficulty, I raised my eyes to Dr. Patten's face. He wasn't smiling, but he also wasn't dialing Battalion HQ.

"Jeff, listen carefully to what I'm going to say. You've just admitted to me that you've made a mistake, perhaps a serious mistake. It doesn't matter what kind or degree, because all of us make them. And, despite the fact that you've made a mistake, I can still tell you with complete assurance that I like you, that I respect your honesty and courage, and that I think you are a person of worth."

I was learning that Dr. Tom Patten was someone I could absolutely trust. He was a naval officer, yet I felt complete confidence in him. I'd never experienced that combination before. I knew if I could become the type of officer he was, I'd be proud to wear the uniform. And, with his help, it just might be possible for me to become whole enough to do it.

For the first time in my life, I began to have hope—even confidence. I felt like a little kid with a new hammer; I was nailing everything in sight. Doc gave me some things to think about, some inner responses and keys to apply to situations that had intimidated and defeated me before.

He gave me some techniques to deal with my feelings of nervousness and anxiety. He showed me how I could put the brakes on my runaway emotions and help myself relax, one muscle at a time. He helped me imagine situations where I might be prone to panic, and helped me understand that the feelings of arousal I experienced in those situations were normal and healthy, rather than bad or shameful. I began to understand that the things the babysitter had done to me when I was four were not related to the behaviors of normal, healthy, consenting adults. Dr. Patten helped me give myself permission to feel sensations of sexual attraction without being guilty or afraid.

The one unknown variable in the equation was Angie. After all, she had needs too! She had the same desire for physical affection and romance as any normal, healthy woman. But, as long as she was with me, she was going to have to postpone the emotional fulfillment she had every right to expect. Would she be able to hang in there without any assurance of ultimate success?

I would learn over the next few weeks and months that Angie was more patient, forbearing, and giving than I had any right to expect. She cared so much about me that she was willing not only to endure but even to encourage my slow, hesitant journey toward emotional health. In many ways, her love saved my life.

I could also see other visible results of my dawning self-assurance: my grades were up, I was more willing to participate openly in class discussions, I was less fearful of expressing my opinions to my peers and I suddenly realized I didn't have to go partying and bar-hopping to feel good about myself. I was coming to terms with the real Jeff Gantar and finding out he wasn't such a bad guy, after all.

I remember discussing with Doc the difficulty of telling my parents about the abusive incident. Christmas break was coming up and I knew I'd have to face the music at home. It would be tough, but now I knew that just because something was difficult didn't mean it should be avoided. I was coming to the realization that telling the truth is the most therapeutic thing you can do for yourself.

After I got home at Christmas, I spent two days sweating bullets about how to tell my parents. On the third day, I was in the car with Mom, going to pick up my sister from her dance class. We had left early to stop at the grocery store. I remember turning toward her, feeling as if I had a tennis ball stuck in my throat. "Mom, I have to tell you something," I croaked.

She looked at me, startled by the sound of my voice, and even more startled to see tears coursing down my cheeks. "Jeff, what is it, honey? What's the matter?"

I told her the whole story. She was very nurturing, as I guess I knew she would be. I suppose that's why I told her first; deep inside, I knew Mom would be accepting, loving, and safe. It was like a fifty-pound weight was lifted off my chest—but I'd started with a hundred pounds. I still had Dad to go.

That night there was a beautifully clear winter sky, more stars than you could imagine, and they looked close enough to grab. Mom, Dad, and I were all sitting in the hot tub in the backyard. There was a long moment of silence, and Mom looked from me to Dad. "Mark," she said slowly, "Jeff has something he needs to tell you."

Will he hate me? I asked myself. The old vestiges of self-doubt were starting to whisper their lies once again. After all, this was my dad, my image of manhood, the one whose approval meant absolutely everything. Will he despise my weakness? Will he still care for me after he knows?

Mom began talking, giving him the main points. I filled in as many details as I could in between sobs. You'd think after telling the story three times, I'd be able to at least get through it once more. But this was different. This was Dad.

When he heard everything, there were a few seconds of quiet, just the rolling and bubbling of the water jets in the hot tub. Then, I felt his arms encircling me. I grabbed him like a life buoy, and he held me for a long time. "Jeff, that's . . . it's horrible, just an incredibly awful thing," he said in a dazed, faraway voice. "I don't know what to do or say." After another long silence, he said, "Son, we'll get you anything you need, do anything to help."

I felt the warm rush of his love; it was like a steak dinner to a starving man. "You don't have to do anything, Dad," I said, my voice still taut with emotion. "Just be there for me."

His only response was to squeeze me a little tighter.

When I hit the rack that night, my mind was spinning. I still could hardly believe I had revealed the ugliest sore on my soul to the four people in the world whose reaction had the power to heal—or destroy. Not only had they not rejected me, they had actually embraced me, affirming me in a way that went beyond anything I had led myself to expect. I laid my head on the pillow, feeling as if I could sleep as soundly as a newborn baby.

And then, I remembered: Double-E—the other untidy little secret I had to deal with.

As difficult as it was to admit the abuse, I could at least now believe that I wasn't to blame. But I couldn't say the same about Double-E. My family had been accepting and supporting of the scared four-year-old who was, in every sense, a victim. How would they feel about the twenty-year-old midshipman who knew he was taking a compromised exam and failed to report it? Who lied repeatedly to cover his butt?

And, yet—in some ways, I was a victim there, too. Who knew that Rounds' "really good gouge" was going to be the real McCoy?

By the time I knew what had happened, the test was already in front of me and everybody else who was in our room that night. What was I supposed to do . . . turn myself in and thereby screw the other guys who participated as unwittingly as I had? Sure, lying was dishonorable—but so was bilging. NIG and the Academy administration had let it be known that those who cooperated might have a chance to graduate. I knew a lot of guys had lied about their own involvement, then turned right around and fingered everyone they could think of, trying to save their own skins.

And, after all, the whole Academy atmosphere was one big whitewash. If I had learned anything in my three-and-a-half years, it was how to look just good enough to get by. What about guys who had not only lied, but intimidated and threatened others into covering for them? Who had only gotten off the hook because they knew someone important? Why should I step in front of a freight train while those guys stood on the side and laughed?

But, wait. When the babysitter violated me, she implanted a lie that grew like a cancer for the next sixteen years. It almost killed me, would have killed me if not for the miracle that allowed me to remember and the courage and understanding that Doc and Angie displayed when they helped me crawl out of the pit.

No, I was done living with lies. I had tasted freedom for the first time in my life, and there was no way I could go back to the stale, bleak slavery of pretense and denial. I wasn't sure what the truth would cost, but I knew it had to be less expensive than continued deceit.

In the days before my return to the Yard, I knew I had to prepare my father for the coming storm. I was looking forward to that conversation about like a nice, slow root canal. But I knew it had to be done, and putting it off wouldn't make it any easier. One evening I went in and sat down across the den from him. I took a deep breath, like a basketball player about to attempt the game-winning free throw with no time left on the clock.

"Dad, I need to talk to you about something."

"Yeah, Jeff. What?"

"Dad, I, ah . . . Back last year, when I was having my problems at the Academy, I—" How to say it? Dad, I screwed up so bad that I might get kicked out of the Academy. Is that the best you can do, Gantar? Think!

"Dad, there was . . . a situation that came up, and—"

"Just get to the point, son."

"Well, umm . . . There was a test that was, ah, compromised—"

"Compromised? What are you talking about?"

"A copy of the test was stolen and passed around prior to—"

"Jeff, what in the . . . You're not telling me you stole a test—"

"No! I didn't steal the test!"

"Well, then, what's this got to do with you?" His face was getting redder and redder. How was I ever going to get through this?

"Dad, a guy stole the test and brought it to our room. We didn't know it was the test, we just thought it was gouge. We studied it and worked the problems like we'd done a hundred times on other tests. But the next morning during the exam, I realized it was the actual test we'd had."

"Why didn't you say something right then? Before the situation went any further?"

Because you rate what you skate, Dad. Because nobody at the Yard cares about your intentions or your circumstances—only how it looks. Because I thought I might shaft the other guys who were in the room with me. Because I had about fifteen seconds to make a decision that might affect the rest of my life. Because, because, because . . .

"I don't know, Dad. I should have gone to the prof, but I didn't."

"Jeff, I can't believe you're in trouble again! After all we went through with you last year, all the frustration and warnings—" He stopped talking, so incensed he couldn't speak.

"Dad, I—I'm really sorry—"

He just shook his head. If he thinks it's bad now, wait till he gets a load of this—

"Dad, I've been twisting back and forth on this thing for a year now, and I've got to get it out in the open. I can't keep covering it up any longer."

He jerked up to look at me. "Jeff? You're not thinking of incriminating yourself, are you?"

Bingo. "Dad, I know what I've got to do, okay?"

"Jeff, listen to me! The Navy doesn't give a plugged nickel about your honesty! All they're after is a tidy package and covered backsides! If you get up there and give them a target, they'll nail you to the wall! Listen to me, son, I know a little about the military—"

"Dad, I can't! I can't go on lying anymore! Lying is what screwed me up in the first place! How can more lying help me now?"

"Jeff, you're not hearing me. I didn't say you should lie. All I said was you shouldn't implicate yourself unnecessarily! The Academy screwed up and didn't take enough precautions with their test; it got out early and probably hundreds of mids had it."

No argument there.

"They're trying to punish a few who accidentally happened upon a copy of the test. Didn't you say you didn't even know what it was when the guy brought it in? See? You didn't do anything that was all that bad. I'm not going to allow my son to be the one who suffers for someone else's mistake! You just hang tight, and we'll get a lawyer, get your grandfather's friends to call and write in—"

"Dad, no! I don't want a lawyer. This is a black-and-white issue for me. I believe I have to take this thing head-on. I just think it's the right thing to do."

He didn't say anything for a long time. Finally, he took a deep breath, held it a couple of seconds, and let it out, slowly. "I disagree, son," he said. "But we can talk more when the time comes."

When the time comes . . . On the flight back to Annapolis, those words echoed through my head. What if I don't graduate? That will kill my parents—not to mention Grandpa. Is it really worth it, just to say I told the truth?

Yes! You can't allow yourself to get derailed from the correct course by anything or anyone—no matter how much you love and care about that cause or person. Don't get enticed by worrying about what might happen. Just put one foot in front of the other and stick to the facts.

Then another troubling thought surfaced: How could I be truthful and avoid bilging? It was one thing to make a decision that had career implications for me, but how could I justify taking a course of action that might drag someone else into my spotlight? All I wanted was to tell the truth. I wasn't doing it to save my skin, and I didn't want to hurt anyone else by doing so. Would I be forced to sacrifice loyalty on the altar of honor?

I began to wonder: Could I convince my friends to do the right thing with me? Could I possibly persuade Brian and the other guys that it was best to come clean about the whole thing, to get it off our chests once and for all? Knowing someone else—anyone else!—was going into battle with me would make it seem easier, I thought.

As for incriminating anyone else, I decided I would just tell what I did, what I saw, and let the brass worry about quizzing the others. If they asked me whether so-and-so was in my room, I would have to answer factually. If they asked me whether he saw the test, I would tell them to ask him themselves.

But what about Brian? He's had top grades and top performance the whole time at the Yard. If anyone deserves to graduate and become an officer, Brian does! What if I do talk him into telling the truth and, as a result, he gets separated? What if he gets kicked out, and I get retained? Could I accept a commission, knowing I was as guilty as he?

Just stick to the facts, Jeff. You can't allow yourself to speculate or take responsibility for what the Navy might or might not do. Just tell the truth. It's the only way. Your only chance.

Not one of my more enjoyable flights, I must say. It was an internal wrestling match, all the way from Spokane to Baltimore. I'm surprised the captain didn't turn on the seat belt signs, with all the heavy weather I was generating.

Angie met me at the airport. As soon as I saw her, I felt the magnitude of the risk increase threefold. What if she despises me? She didn't sign on for this!

Driving back to her apartment, I told her a little bit about the Double-E, a few of the details of my involvement.

"Jeff, I really don't want to know any more about it," she told me, finally. "I trust you, and I think you have to do what you think is right."

"Angie, I just wanted you to know that things could get . . . could get pretty tough for me when it all goes down."

The look in her eyes made me stop breathing. "Jeff, I'll be here, no matter what," she said. Does she really mean that? I wondered. Does she really know what she's saying? I prayed to God she did and would. I felt like she was the anchor to everything. She was the one who had gotten everything out of me and had brought me closer to myself and to God. And I would have done anything for her.

Later on Angie would tell me that she was scared to death. She said she tried to believe in me, but she was really frightened that it was all going to come crashing down around us.

Classes resumed the following Monday. And I knew I had to tell Dr. Patten. I had come to trust him implicitly, to regard him less as counselor than as friend. I earnestly wanted his advice about the best way to ride out the hurricane in my immediate future.

Still . . . I'd never really spelled out to him the shape of my dilemma. No one meant more to me than my dad, and things hadn't exactly gone swimmingly in our conversations on this subject. And Dr. Patten was, after all, a career Navy man!

But it had to be done. I made an appointment, and that afternoon I went to the Counseling Center.

☆ 13 ☆

THE
HOT SEAT

Tom

I WAS GLAD TO see Jeff, but within about ten seconds I could tell it would be another interesting session. All the signs were there: the tense look, the darting eyes, the anemic smile of greeting. Jeff had something on his heart, and I was going to hear it. Given our recent experiences together, I made sure I had a good grip on the seat of my chair when he started talking. I wasn't disappointed.

"Doc, you know I told you once I had committed an honor violation."

"Yes, I remember. And I also remember I said that just because you'd made a mistake didn't mean I regarded you as a lost cause."

"Yeah." A quick smile, a glance at me, then back into the brown study. "Well, I need to tell you that . . . I was involved in the Double-E thing."

The last phrase had come out in a rush of words. It was a second or two before the sounds had coalesced into a coherent image in my mind. But coalesce they did.

I forced my voice to remain neutral. "Involved?"

"Uh, yeah. One of the guys somehow got a copy of the exam and brought it to my room the night before the test. I thought it was gouge at first, but the next morning I knew it was the test." He couldn't look at me now. His eyes were fastened on his shoes, and his knuckles showed white where he gripped his fists in his lap.

"Well, Jeff, in all fairness, I suppose I shouldn't be too surprised. I know a lot of guys were involved, and I guess it might have been pretty easy to get bitten by the Double-E bug." There was a long silence.

I kept a set of metal stress reliever balls on my desk. You could roll them around in your palm and they made a soft, musical jingling sound. Jeff reached over and grabbed them, and in the funeral parlor hush of my office it began to sound like Santa Claus was comin' to town.

The Question was looming huge between us. Eventually, I had to ask. "Jeff," I said softly, "look at me." Reluctantly, his eyes rose to meet mine. "What are you going to do?"

"What do you think I should do?"

And suddenly my toes were again hanging over the edge of the chasm, staring into the depths of my own dark night of the soul. Okinawa . . . The master chief's alcoholism profile . . . "Tom, give the CO what he wants" . . . Passed over twice for promotion . . . Out of the Navy, effective 1 September 1994 . . . Lie and survive? Or tell the truth and accept the consequences? God, what do I tell this kid?

"Jeff, I can't tell you what to do." Now I was having trouble looking him in the eye. "No matter what you decide, it won't be easy. But I'll tell you this—" I managed to fix him with a rigid stare. "No matter what, I will stand by you."

His spine seemed to stiffen when I said that. "Doc, I'm going to confess. I can't lie anymore. Not about this—not about anything."

I took a deep breath. *May God help you, Jeff.* "Okay. How do you think you'll go about it?"

"I . . . I don't know. I want to get everything out in the open, but I don't want to bilge anyone."

"Jeff, that'll be tough. A lot of guys are involved. It's going to be tricky."

He nodded sadly. After a moment's reflection, he said, more to himself than to me, "If only I could get the other guys to do the right thing, too. I think I can convince Brian; he's a good guy. I don't want to go through this thing alone. But I will if I have to."

"When do you think you should do it?"

"I've thought about that a lot, too. I could run to the commandant right now and spill my guts, but I don't want it to look like I'm trying to save my hide or tell on anyone else. This mustn't look like an attempt at self-preservation. Megan Merriman named about fifty mids whom she guessed had the test. She named me, Doc, and I barely even know her. I sure didn't see her the night before the Double-E. I want everyone to know that I'm doing this because it's right, not because I'm trying to get off the hook. If the Navy graduates me, it has to be on my true merits as a person and an officer, not because I ratted out my friends or made some kind of plea bargain."

I felt amazement blooming in my mind. This kid was displaying a bravery and a maturity that bordered on being breathtaking. All I could do was nod and wait for him to continue.

"No, I don't think I should do anything right now. I think I should wait for my honor board to talk about it. Maybe it's not the best timing as far as graduation, but I think it's the right thing to do."

Eventually, I found my voice. "Jeff, I'm very, very proud and moved by what you've said. You have the highest sense of honor, and I sincerely hope the Navy sees that and gives you the hearing you deserve."

We shook hands and he left the office, his posture ramrod-straight and a glint of determination in his eye. As the door closed behind him, I leaned on my elbows and cupped my face in my hands. *I hope he's dealt a better hand than I got. He deserves it.*

JEFF: The naval investigator-general's report came out in mid January, 1994. It listed 134 mids as having probable involvement, including me, Brian, and all the other guys in our room that night. A panel of Navy officers was convened to review NIG's findings and recommend those named whom they believed deserved closer scrutiny. The panel dropped the cases against nineteen mids and recommended the rest for hearing before special honor boards conducted by Rear Admiral R. C. Allen, who had been brought in by the secretary of the Navy to impose order upon the chaos created by Superintendent Lynch's botched efforts.

Just after NIG's report was released, I decided the time was right to talk to Brian. One evening after tables, we were in our quarters studying for some exam or other. For what seemed like half an hour, I stared at the back of his head, bent dutifully over the pile of opened books and scattered class notes in front of him. Finally, I cleared my throat. I used my patented Double-E opening line:

"Hey, uh . . . Brian. I need to talk to you about something."

"Yeah, what is it?" he mumbled, his eyes fastened on his books, his left index finger scrolling down a column of figures while he scribbled notes with his right hand.

"It's, uh—it's about the Double-E, Bri." Taking a firm grip on the cement block, I stepped off the wharf and into the icy water. "I think I'm going to confess."

"Yeah, right," he snickered, still scrawling in his notebook. "And Braswell's up for the Nobel Peace Prize."

"Brian, listen, man! I'm serious. I don't think I can keep up the lies, and if I get called in for an honor board, I'm going to tell them the truth—what really happened."

He put down his pencil in slow motion, just as slowly turned in his chair to face me. He stared at me, and I willed my eyes to lock onto his, willed myself not to flinch away from the appraising, unbelieving, shocked expression on his features.

"You really mean it." It wasn't a question.

"Yeah, Bri. A lot of things have become clearer for me, since I've been seeing Dr. Patten, and one of them is that I can't allow myself to continue a way of life that's based on lies and dishonesty. It'll kill me if I try to keep it up, and ... I've decided I just have to put this thing behind me, once and for all." There were thousands more words I wanted to say, but I clenched my jaws against them and gave him a chance to speak. Brian had stood beside me when it was neither popular nor strategic. How would he react to me now? He crossed his arms on his chest and stared out the darkened window for about twenty heartbeats. Then he looked back at me.

"Jeff, you know what'll happen to you if you confess, don't you?"

I shrugged. "Yeah, I think so. But—"

"Let me just make sure you understand, buddy," he interrupted. "Let's look at your scorecard, okay? First," he said, holding up a finger, "your grades are nothing to brag about, certainly not what you're capable of. Agreed?"

I shrugged again, and nodded.

"Second, your military record, up until this year, is somewhat less than stellar. Right so far?"

My silence was the only confirmation he needed.

"Third, you've got no leverage. You're not a varsity athlete anymore, Jeff. Why should they cut you any slack, once you offer them your jugular? Fourth, and most deadly of all, Braswell still hasn't forgotten about you. You confess, and you're dead meat, man."

I dragged my eyes up to meet his. "I don't care about that, Brian. Sure, I want to graduate; I want it so bad I can taste it, just like everybody else here. But ..." How to say it, without sounding like a Sunday school teacher? "Brian, there's something more important than getting a piece of paper and a gold stripe on your shoulderboards. There's ... honor. The personal, private feeling of knowing, no matter what it cost you, that you did the one-hundred-percent right thing. That's what I'm after, Bri. Honor. Not as defined by the Academy, not by Brazz, not Lynch, not by anybody else but me. If I can't find inside myself what it means to be a person of honor, then . . ." I looked at him, willing the tears not to spill down my cheeks. " . . . then what difference does the Navy make, anyway?"

There was a long silence, punctuated only by the faraway sounds of boats on the Severn River and in the city harbor. Finally, I heard a deep breath whoosh out from between his lips. "Okay," he said, running his hand through his hair, "so you're going to put your neck in the noose. Why are you telling me?"

"Because I want you to join me on the scaffold," I said, a wan half smile flickering on, then off. "Because I want you to do the right thing, too."

He chuckled and looked away, shaking his head. "Why am I not surprised?"

I figured if he was going to cold cock me he would have already done it, so I kept talking. "Brian, you're my best friend. You hung in with me during the tough times, when Brazz was gunning for me and anybody that looked like me. I had to tell you, Brian—I couldn't afford for you to believe I would betray your trust. But I hoped you'd see that what I'm saying is right; that it's wrong to graduate only because we weren't willing to come forward and tell the truth. And if we get separated and walk away from here with nothing but our dignity and our personal honor, then—I'm saying that's enough."

"But what about the other guys, Jeff? What about Jason? He was crying during that last time with NIG. He's half crazy, worrying about what his family will think if he's separated—"

Grandpa . . . The sword . . . My dad . . .

"And what about Jon and Terry? They'll never talk! They've practically got 'Lie Till You Die' tattooed on their chests! Those guys will never see it your way."

"Maybe not, but it doesn't matter. They've got to live with what they did, and so do I. This is how I choose to do it."

We talked and hashed and rehashed for about four hours. Brian was right about one thing, and I knew it, deep down: with his grades and record, he might have an outside shot at being retained, even if he told the truth—for me, things were much more grim. But, somehow, a small, inner voice kept telling me I was on the right track for once in my life. That voice told me I shouldn't worry about what Jon and Terry thought—or even Brian. Because I respected and appreciated him so much, I badly wanted Brian to come around to my way of thinking. But even if he didn't, I knew what I was going to do.

It was after midnight, and we'd about unraveled the whole thing and knitted it back together again. Brian looked at me, and said, "Okay, Jeff. I'm in."

I stared at him. "Brian? Are you sure, man? You know what may happen."

"Yeah, I know. But I also know you're right; we stonewalled this thing just like everybody else, and it wasn't right. We've got to face the music. I'm with you."

I slept more soundly that night than I had in weeks.

To no one's surprise, everyone who was in our room on that fateful night received notice of an upcoming Allen Board—Yard slang for the special honor boards to be chaired by Rear Admiral Allen. The real kidney punch came when I received my disclosure of the evidence that had been presented against me: four of the guys who were in the room that night, four of the guys who, with the rest of us, had entered on a solemn pact not to bilge each other—had stated they believed Brian and I had the test.

When the NIG investigators told me my friends had told on me, I didn't believe it. I knew those guys wouldn't go back on their word, knew they wouldn't bilge. But there it was, in black and white: Two of them had stated their own innocence but had alleged my guilt and Brian's. They had ratted us out! They were trying to climb over us to save themselves! It turned out that they had made incriminating statements against us all the way back in September, 1993. For five months, they had allowed Brian and me to believe they were standing firm, keeping their word. And all the time, they knew they had bilged us! Jon Moore had even gone so far as to state I was not his friend, that he didn't really know me all that well.

I was hurt deeply. Not that it made any difference in what I intended; I was just as determined as ever to do what I had to do. But it wounded my heart to know that people who called themselves friends were capable of such duplicity.

Eventually, Brian and I could laugh about it. These guys were lying about us, assuming that we would continue to deny everything and keep the trail sufficiently muddied to allow us all to slip through—or at least to allow them to slip through. The irony was that none of the statements were likely to be sufficiently damning to make separation a foregone conclusion. Only an outright confession would do that.

When I had the date for my Allen Board, I knew I had to call my dad. I dreaded that phone call more than any call I'd ever made—more even than telling Grandpa I was on restriction.

Each time we'd talked since my return from Christmas, Dad would ask about the Double-E affair. He'd want to know what was happening, what I'd heard, what I planned to do. He continued to urge me not to incriminate myself, urged me to let him get a lawyer—anything he could think of to protect his son from being hurt further by a system he perceived as corrupt and hypocritical.

I just listened. I knew he wanted me to keep quiet, but I knew that wasn't an option for me. It tore me up inside to go against my dad, but I didn't see any other way.

When I called to tell him about my Allen Board, it was more of the same. "Let me get an attorney, Jeff! At the very least, you're entitled to legal counsel in this situation that will drastically affect the rest of your life! Let me talk to Dad. He knows lots of people in Washington—"

"No, Dad! I can't play it that way!"

"Why not, Jeff? Why do you insist on punishing yourself beyond anything you deserve? Never in your life have you been a quitter, Jeff. Why are you choosing this moment to start?"

After such conversations, I felt as if my nerves were on a rack, being ratcheted tighter and tighter—to the breaking point. Sometimes, I thought maybe I really was crazy—or terminally quixotic. Maybe Dad was right, maybe I should just keep my mouth shut and see if the whole thing would blow over . . .

But that inner voice wouldn't leave me alone. It kept reminding me that truth was wholeness, truth was healing, truth was the only way out. Not the easy way—just the only way.

I felt as if I were standing on a lonely precipice, staring down at a world I no longer knew or understood. Up to this point in my life, I had lived and breathed to earn the approval of those who mattered most to me. My whole existence had been bound up in figuring out what they wanted, and giving it to them. But now, the rules had changed, the pole star had shifted. I had come to understand that my ultimate responsibility was to myself, the way I was on the inside. It was no longer enough to have the acceptance of other people: I had to be able to accept myself, to know that what the outside world saw was consistent with who I really was.

Deep down, I knew my dad wasn't actually angry with me. He was angry at a situation that was poised to deeply wound his son. His frustration was increased, I think, by my apparent unwillingness to take measures of self-preservation that seemed to him to be appropriate, given the circumstances. It hurt him to see me get hurt, and I think the only way he knew to express that hurt was to urge me to do something I didn't feel I should do. He was trying to protect me from what I had done to myself, but I had come to the conclusion that if I was ever to be whole and genuine, I could no longer afford such protection. This was a gauntlet I had to pass on my own.

Doctor Patten seemed to understand this. He never once tried to tell me what I should do or say. At times, I almost had the sense he had experienced a similar dilemma. He was unfailingly supportive of my decision and of me as a person. I never felt I was on shaky ground with him, and I was more grateful for his consistency than I'll ever be able to express.

22 March 1993: the Day of Reckoning. That was the date set for my Allen Board. I felt I had a responsibility to the other guys in our room that night to tell them what I was going to do at my board. Some of them probably didn't deserve it, but I believed I should let them know I didn't plan to continue the deception. Some of them felt so guilty about bilging Brian and me on their statements to NIG that they wouldn't have objected to anything I wanted to do—no matter how crazy they thought it might be. They apologized all over themselves, even admitting they had hoped I wouldn't see their NIG testimony and know what they'd said.

Jon Moore's Allen Board was scheduled to take place a few days before my own, and the night before, he came to my quarters to coach me on what he wanted me to say. He knew what I was planning to do at my own board, and, needless to say, I wasn't his star witness. If he'd had his own way, I probably wouldn't have gotten an invitation to his little clambake. But since his own NIG testimony had placed him in my quarters the night before the Double-E, there was no question of my being absent from the proceedings.

I knew what he was going to ask me to do, and I knew he wouldn't be a happy camper when he left. Still, I dreaded the confrontation. Jon had been a good friend at one time, notwithstanding what he'd said to NIG.

"Jeff, I want to ask you some of the questions I'll be asking you tomorrow, okay?"

"Jon, we've been through this already—"

"Yeah, yeah, I know. If you want to torpedo your career, that's your business. But I don't plan on going down with you. Now, are you going to let me ask these questions, or not?"

I sighed and shrugged. "Sure, Jon. Fire away."

"Okay. Now, first, I'm going to ask how it was that I came to study with you that night. What will you say?"

"Well, we started talking at muster and you told me you had a D in EE311, and you were really worried about the exam. I told you I had a strong B and Brian had an A and we would be glad to help you on any problems you wanted. I also told you that Rounds was supposed to be bringing some really good gouge, and you said you'd drop by after my restriction muster."

"Yeah, that's good, that's good!" he grinned, scribbling notes on a legal pad. "I'm gonna beat this thing, yet, man! Okay, now . . . I want you to tell the board that I was only in your room about half an hour, or maybe less—"

"Sorry, Jon," I interrupted, shaking my head. "No can do. You were there until about 0300, just like everyone else. I'm not going to lie for you, Jon—"

"Jeff, what are you talking about? You've been lying all along, up till now! I swear, if you bilge me, I'll—"

"I'm not going to bilge you, Jon! I'm just not going to say something untrue to help you get off the hook. And, besides, if you want to talk about bilging, how about your little performance for NIG?"

For an instant, he looked like a cat with canary feathers sticking out of his mouth. Then he blew up. "Fine, then! If you want to do something crazy, just go right ahead, man!"

I looked away, not bothering to answer. He stomped out, slamming the door behind him. A couple of minutes later, I heard the door creak open, followed by Jon's voice. "Hey, Jeff, I'm sorry, man. I shouldn't have lost it like that."

I didn't say anything. He edged farther into the room. "Look, I don't want you to lie, okay? But . . . Just don't say I was in the room with Rounds. Don't bring it up that he hit me up for money for the test, all right? It would really look bad. Just don't mention it. Whaddya say?"

I grimaced and ran my hand through my hair. "Listen, Jon. I'm not going to turn you in. I'm not going to tell the board what you saw. I'm going to tell them what I saw. If they want to know what was in your head, they're going to have to ask you themselves." I saw him start to smile and relax, but I knew I wasn't finished yet.

"But, Jon, I'm going to stick to the facts—the real ones. I am honor-bound to truthfully answer any question they ask. Jon, we were all working the same problems. If the Allen Board asks me whether I think you saw the test or whether I think you're guilty, I'm going to tell them to ask you. That's the best I can do for you, Jon. I wish you and Terry would just tell the truth."

I saw his jaw clenching in anger. "Thanks, pal," he muttered between his teeth, "for nothing. I'm gonna graduate from this joint, and you and your sweet little honest friends are going to get your tails booted out, and then where will your self-righteous crap take you?"

Brian edged past him into the room, staring quizzically at the two of us. Jon spun on his heel and stomped out. "Later. Pirko, I can't believe you're letting this guy take you down with him."

"Whatever, Jon," Brian shot back. "It's the right thing to do, and you know it!"

"Yeah, right," he flung over his shoulder. Then he was gone.

THE ALLEN
BOARDS

THE ALLEN BOARDS CONVENED at 0730 each morning in a large conference room, commonly known as the Boardroom, on the main floor of Alumni Hall. The room was furnished in a sleek, modern style contrasting with the Victorian appearance of many rooms at the Academy. There was lots of wood paneling, and new blue carpet had been laid not long before the Allen Boards began—the scent was unmistakable.

When you walked in, the first thing you saw was a long table on a raised dais with five chairs behind it, flanked by two American flags—the board members' table. You sat at a smaller table, looking up at the board, accompanied by your counsel. Any witnesses sat at another small table to the right of the accused, between the board's table and that of the accused, facing the center of the room. To the left of the accused was the recorder—like a stenographer in a courtroom. I remember walking into Jon's board and looking over at him, realizing I would be seated where he was in about forty-eight hours. I sat down and waited for my cue. Admiral Allen looked over at me and began speaking.

"Midshipman, for the record, please state your full name, spelling your last name."

"Jeffrey Dorian Gantar, G-A-N-T-A-R."

"Thank you, Mister Gantar. Mister Moore has made certain statements regarding his actions on the night of 13 December 1992. You are instructed to hear his questions and answer them truthfully to the best of your ability. Do you understand?"

"Yes, Sir."

Jon cleared his throat, shuffled his notes nervously, and started speaking. I noticed he never made eye contact with me.

"Mr. Gantar, isn't it true that I never actually saw the compromised exam for EE311, and that in fact, I was only in your room that night for about thirty minutes?"

I shook my head. He just didn't get it! "I'm sorry, Mr. Moore, but you were in my room for at least three hours and copied solutions to several problems. I cannot specifically state whether you saw the test, but it was in plain view all during the time you were in the room, and everyone there was working on it."

Admiral Allen's eyes bulged at Jon; then he swiveled to face me. "Mister Gantar, you realize that Mister Moore has stated that he never saw the test in question. In your opinion, did he see the test?"

I took a deep breath. "Sir, I would prefer not to give my opinion on that matter, since I cannot categorically say what Mister Moore did or did not see. I was not inside his mind that night, Sir. I can say that I saw the test and assumed that everyone else in the room did, also. I helped Mister Moore work several problems, which is why he came to the room. I do not wish to take responsibility for his answers, however, and I respectfully request that the question of having seen the test be put to him directly, since he alone knows with certainty what he did or did not see."

Before anyone else could speak, Jon launched hurriedly into his next question.

"Mister Gantar, isn't it true that I left your room before Chris Rounds arrived and began asking for money?"

I stared directly at him as I replied. "Jon, you were definitely in the room when Rounds started asking people for money."

It went on like that for quite a while: Jon tossing out leading questions; me refusing to follow. I could see the color rising in his cheeks, and if we hadn't been in front of a rear admiral, three captains, and a Marine Corps colonel, he would probably have strangled me with my web belt.

Jon's testimony began to smell like rotten Limburger. I was excused before it got really ugly, but I heard they ripped him a new one after I left. Still, I have to hand it to Jon: he stuck to his story, clung to it like a shipwrecked sailor clings to a splintered beam. They couldn't break him.

A couple of days later, it was my turn. I walked back into that conference room, but this time I sat in the place of the accused.

I was feeling more alone than ever before in my life. The night before, Dad and I had talked by phone. Probably a mistake. He was furious with me for not allowing him to bring in an attorney or mobilize Grandpa's influence. My endurance was stretched so thin I could barely breathe, and finally it became too much.

"Dad, I'm going to do what I think is right, no matter what you say!" I yelled into the phone. "I may be stupid and foolish and everything else, but this is my problem and this is how I'm going to resolve it." I slammed the phone into the cradle and stalked away. I had hung up on my dad.

I lay awake for most of that night, feeling completely wretched. I hung up on my own father! I'll probably be separated—everything he says will happen. I'll lose his respect, Grandpa's—maybe even Angie's!

Angie still couldn't believe the Academy would really kick me out for cheating. I didn't have the heart or the guts to make her see how serious my situation was. Instead, we'd begun to talk about how life would be after I graduated, after I got my commission and my duty station in San Diego. She'd begun to read brochures about San Diego and we'd even started talking about marriage, discussed possible dates. I suppose I was living in a fantasy world—one I desperately wished could become real.

But all that was about to come crashing down, starting at 0730 in the morning. For about the millionth time, I asked myself, "Is it worth it?" I knew I could avoid all the unpleasantness simply by telling the Allen Board the same sort of things Jon and scores of others had told them. They might rip into me, might grill me and catch me in gross inconsistencies, but if the past was any indication, they wouldn't separate me without an outright confession. As long as I didn't openly admit guilt, I could keep from breaking everyone's heart, could keep all the dreams alive—for myself, for Angie, for Dad and Grandpa . . .

That night was a lonely vigil. I don't think I slept more than a couple of hours, if that. I rolled out early, though; bathed and shaved and got my uniform in spotless condition. If I have to go down in flames, I thought, at least I can look like a champion . . .

At 0731, my Allen Board was called to order by Rear Admiral Allen, the presiding officer. Trying desperately to avoid eye contact, I studied the members of the board. To my far left was Captain Lee Womack, a man with close-cropped hair and wire-rimmed glasses, which he wore low on the bridge of his nose, lending him a bookish, almost academic air. His face was impassive and would remain so through the entire proceeding. To his left was Captain William Sutton. Sutton was tall and thin, with short, immaculately-combed gray hair. His face betrayed more interest and emotion than Captain Womack's, and he seemed to be genuinely interested in what was said and done—even sympathetic at times. On my far right was

Marine Colonel William Jones. He was tall and stocky, with a face as rugged and durable as chiseled granite. To his right was Captain Barbara McGann, a middle-aged woman of medium height, with a round, sensitive face and short brown hair. I sensed immediately that she was the most caring and empathetic member of the board.

In the center, of course, sat Rear Admiral R. C. Allen, the presiding officer. Admiral Allen appeared to be in his sixties, and possessed an air of sturdiness and strength, like a weathered tree trunk. Still, in the midst of that sea- and wind-hardened face were eyes that hinted at a center of warmth and compassion.

Lieutenant James Secor, from the Judge-Advocate General Corps, acted as counsel to the board, and Lieutenant Commander Julie Tinker was my counsel. In that capacity, she could assist and advise me, but she could not present my case nor address the board.

As I fidgeted at the table and waited for the proceedings to begin, I remembered the semicomical scene when I had told Lieutenant Commander Tinker of my intention to plead guilty to cheating and lying. After she picked her jaw up off the table, she dragged out the two-inch-thick stack of forms she had been using at other boards and started pulling out papers. "Well, in that case, we won't need this," she said, yanking out a form and tossing it aside, "or this, or this, or this . . ." She was so accustomed to mids coming in and pleading "not guilty," she was totally unprepared for me.

"Midshipman Gantar, you are called before this Honor Review Board because you have been charged with cheating and lying," Admiral Allen was saying, "formal notification of such charges having been delivered to you in writing on 7 February 1994. Do you understand the charges brought against you?"

Showtime! "Yes, Sir."

"Do you understand the rules that govern this Board, its purposes, and its general function?"

"Yes, Sir."

"Midshipman Gantar, this board is not an adversarial proceeding. It has been assigned its responsibility at the direction of the chief of naval operations. This is not a formal process, but rather a strictly administrative process. Do you understand and agree to this?"

"Yes, Sir."

"Have you been advised of your rights before this board, and do you have any questions about those rights?"

"I have been duly advised, Sir. I have no questions."

I noticed that Admiral Allen's voice sounded tired, drab, disinterested. I suppose that would have been understandable, considering the number of cases he had already heard, and the number he still had to listen to. I'm sure he and the other board members were getting plenty sick of hearing variations on the same old song and dance: "No, Sir, I never saw the test. Yes, Sir, I believe Midshipmen X, Y, and Z may have had the test . . ." This was surely far from enjoyable duty for these officers.

"Very well," he continued. "The record will show that the board has received the following letters from Midshipman Gantar: Request for Presence of Counsel and Delay Request. These letters and the board's response to each will be attached to the record. I can, in good conscience, perform my duties without prejudice or partiality, and render an unbiased vote based solely upon the evidence presented at this hearing. Do each of the other members of the board believe that you can, in good conscience, perform your duties without prejudice or partiality and render an unbiased vote based solely upon the evidence that is presented at this hearing?" Each of the members of the board answered individually in the affirmative.

"Midshipman Gantar, do you have any questions for board members designed to help determine reasons he or she might not be able to hear this case impartially?"

"No, Sir."

"Do you desire to challenge any member for cause?"

"No, Sir."

"Midshipman Gantar, you have a right to a hearing before this board of which any finding of a violation would have to be based on a preponderance of the evidence. You may, however, plead guilty to any or all charges if you so desire. Midshipman Gantar, do you desire to plead guilty to any of the charges?"

I felt my heart banging away at my ribcage, felt as if a fist were shoving into my solar plexus. Here goes. "Yes, Sir, I do."

Admiral Allen's eyebrows lifted a notch. Captain Sutton edged forward in his chair, almost imperceptibly. This has to be a novel experience for them, I thought.

"Which charge or charges do you desire to plead guilty to?" Admiral Allen was asking.

"Sir, the charge of cheating and the charge of lying, Sir."

Admiral Allen reached for the forms Lieutenant Commander Tinker had submitted just before the hearing began. "Midshipman Gantar, you have pled guilty to the charge of cheating, specifically on 14 December 1992, and lying, as charged on 14 January 1993 and 26 August 1993. I have a form that you have signed indicating that you understand the effect of a guilty plea. You also indicate your understanding that by pleading guilty, you are willingly giving up rights that you would have if you did not plead guilty, including the right to remain silent. Do you have any questions about the rights you are giving up by pleading guilty?"

"No, Sir, I don't."

"Do you still desire to plead guilty to both cheating and lying?"

"Yes, Sir, I do." In for a penny, in for a pound.

"I am now going to ask you about the offenses to which you have pled guilty. Lieutenant Secor, would you administer the oath, please?"

The JAG officer had me raise my right hand and swear or affirm to tell the whole truth and nothing but. Then it was Admiral Allen's turn again. He ascertained that I admitted my use of unauthorized assistance to complete the final exam for EE311 on 14 December

1992, and that I admitted lying about it to NIG on 11 January and 26 August, 1993. In excruciating detail, he asked me to verify the events leading up to the final exam and its aftermath, including the details of the ill-fated study session the night before.

Somehow, in the plain, unadorned phrases that the board used, the whole thing sounded much more cut-and-dried, much more obvious than it seemed at the time, that night in my quarters. I had had the naive impression that all I needed to do was come in and say, "I'm guilty," and that would be it. I now realized there were more complex implications than simple guilt or innocence. But I kept going back to my bottom line: I knew something was fishy when Rounds first approached Brian and me, but I failed to take evasive action. Maybe, in my nervousness and haste, I was admitting to more than I strictly had to, but at that moment, I thought it was better to admit to more, rather than to less.

"Did you pay any money for the exam to Midshipman Rounds?" Admiral Allen demanded, at one point. The question sounded hard, almost accusatory. I felt as if they were trying to catch me in a lie or an inconsistency. Also, I knew where some of the impetus for this question came from. A guy named Belding, who had been separated for academics a year and a half ago, had also been deeply involved in Double-E. Belding and I were lab partners in Naval Architecture, and I knew he was struggling academically, including EE311. I offered to help him study for the final, and told him I was getting some good gouge from Rounds. If he wanted to come by the room, I'd help him, I said.

Belding told me no, thanks. His roommate was getting the same stuff as Rounds, he said. Later, when Belding got called in for Double-E, he hypothesized to NCIS that I was involved with Rounds, perhaps even helping him sell copies of the exam. He also named Brian, whom he probably couldn't have recognized in a lineup. I was deeply incensed that Belding had bilged me, and I felt I needed to set the record straight, once and for all.

"No, Sir, I didn't," I replied to the admiral's question.

"Did Mister Pirko?" he shot back.

"I don't believe so, Sir."

"Did you offer to sell the exam to Mister Belding?"

Belding, you jerk! "No, Sir, I did not offer to sell the exam to Mister Belding, Sir!" I gave them the entire scenario, including Belding's refusal of my offer of help, and his comment about the material he would be getting from his roommate.

After a few more questions about the circumstances of the exam and some of the people involved, Admiral Allen asked, "Why did you intentionally provide false answers to NCIS and NIG?"

"Sir, I agreed to cover up with my friends. There's no real excuse for what I did. It was the act of a weak person, and I shouldn't have done it, Sir."

Then Captain McGann asked, "Could you go through the sequence of this agreement on the cover-up and who was involved and how you decided to do this?"

This was tough. She was asking me to make a factual statement about other mids who had agreed with me to conceal the truth. Would I be bilging if I gave names? It wouldn't be hearsay, since I well knew who had talked to Brian and me about Double-E and who hadn't.

Then there was the fact that I had told the people involved what I was going to do here today—absolutely unlike what happened when the other guys, without any warning before or after, rolled over on Brian and me in front of NIG. Moore, Johnson, all the others; they knew what I was going to say. In fact, they'd already had their boards, and I had testified at most of them. I wasn't covering any new ground here. I took a deep breath, looked at all the brass seated on the dais above me, and started talking.

"Everybody in my room decided not to say anything about the compromise of the exam. Midshipman Rounds frequently came in to talk to Midshipman Pirko about what to say and what I should say.

We were all involved, and it wasn't right, but that's what we did, Sir—excuse me, Ma'am—and I didn't speak up as I should have, so—"

"Was the agreement between you and Mister Pirko and Mister Rounds, or was anyone else involved in this agreement?" she interrupted. She wasn't going to get off this track unless I gave her what she wanted. What else could I say?

"Yes, ma'am. Midshipman Berger, Midshipman Barnes, and everybody else was kind of in agreement about keeping quiet being the best thing to do, and when NCIS called me in, Midshipman Rounds advised me not to say anything, that they wouldn't be able to prove anything, and that he would help me out. I went along with this advice and with the wishes of my friends. I didn't want to give them up. I didn't want to deal with their anger at that point in my life. I shouldn't have felt that way, but I did, Ma'am."

One of the other board members asked, "Who was the ringleader of this cover-up policy?"

"Well . . . Midshipman Rounds was covering up from the beginning, because he was being investigated in connection with Midshipman Walker's testimony, although he was talking to Midshipman Pirko more than to me. And all the others were coming to us for advice, and . . ." I spread my hands in a gesture of helplessness. Sir, you rate what you skate! " . . . we said we weren't going to say anything, and they all went along with that." What could be worse than the certainty of falling off Jacob's Ladder? "Everybody was gravely afraid of being separated and disappointing their parents—" Dad. Grandpa. The sword. "—and giving up their friends, and having their friends not like them—" Don't bilge. Your buddies are your lifeline, your key to survival . . . "So . . . no one spoke up, Sir. No one stepped forward and told the truth." No one wanted to bleed in front of the sharks, Sir. No one wanted to swallow the hemlock . . .

"How about Moore and Johnson?" someone else quizzed. "Were they involved in this, also?"

What was with these guys? Was it ever going to stop? "Yes, Sir," I replied, warily. "They came to our room for advice, and we told them we weren't going to say anything, that we were going to deny along with Midshipman Rounds, and they agreed to go along with that, Sir." They wanted into the Holy of Holies, too, Sir. It's the only thing you really learn to hope for, and we were all doing what we thought we had to do . . .

"Any other questions regarding accepting the guilty plea?" Admiral Allen asked, finally. Thank you, God! Let's get back to Jeff and off all those other guys! I was immensely relieved when none of the other board members could think of any more questions.

"Midshipman Gantar, your guilty pleas for lying and cheating are accepted. You've pled guilty to all charges and your pleas have been accepted. On the basis of your pleas, the board finds that you violated the Honor Concept by cheating on 14 December 1992, and lying to the NCIS on 11 January 1993 and to the NIG on 26 August 1993."

Naturally, it was no surprise to hear him say that. Still, the reality of my situation began to feel like a lead weight in my stomach: I was guilty; there would be punishment.

"The board must still determine the disposition of your case, whether to refer your case to the commandant of midshipmen for administrative action or to forward your case to the secretary of the Navy with a recommendation that you be separated from the Naval Academy. In addition to what you've already said and what is in the case file, the board will consider your performance and conduct files. Do you have any objections to the consideration of this material?"

"No, Sir."

After a few more explanations and disclaimers, Admiral Allen announced, "I would like to call in the 25th Company Officer."

Braswell.

I felt like a Thanksgiving turkey, all trussed up and lying on the chopping block. Brazz would be asked to assess my performance and conduct, to provide background for the board as they considered my punishment.

I watched as Brazz stepped into the room, glancing first at me, then at the board. He had a poker face; I couldn't read anything. He sat at the witness table, raised his hand and took the oath administered by Lieutenant Secor, then stated and spelled his name for the record.

One of the board members asked, "Mister Braswell, would you please share with us your thoughts about Midshipman Gantar; what kind of a midshipman he's been in 25th Company, what type of contact you've had with him, how his jobs have been performed, any comments you want to make about his conduct or performance file, any comments you want to make about his personal integrity, his potential for the future, and whether or not you would like to serve with him in our Navy?"

Oh, man! With a straight line like that, how can he miss? Well, Brazz, here's your chance, old pal. I'm sitting in your crosshairs, dead in the water. All you've got to do is push the button . . .

"Yes, Sir," Braswell began. "Midshipman Gantar came to the 25th Company at the same time I did. He ran into conduct trouble his first semester in 25th and did a number of days' restriction—"

. . . Missing Thanksgiving with his grandfather and Christmas with his family . . .

"—and that whole situation seemed to snowball on him for a while—"

Brazz's favorite metaphor.

"—and it did impact his overall performance in the Company."

Yep. I'm scuttled and sunk.

"Mister Gantar never developed a bad attitude from that. He just sort of took his licks and moved on. But all the while that was going on, I personally had questions about how honest he had been in the situation and, in fact, I put him up for an honor offense. That matter was resolved at the commandant's level, being dismissed. There are still questions in my mind as to whether I made the correct call in distrusting him or whether he, in fact, had lied to me. I still haven't resolved that in my mind, but we moved on from there."

What? Do I sense a faint attempt to cut me some slack?

"Midshipman Gantar's performance has improved during this last year. In the past, he has had problems with upholding the standards of the company and setting a good example for the underclass. That has improved tremendously over the last year. His performance as a squad leader the first semester this year was quite good: he maintained a good notebook on all his personnel, and was one of the few squad leaders whom I felt really knew his people and carefully tracked their performance academically, militarily and in their PEP courses. From that perspective, I think he has potential for service in the Navy."

Somebody pinch me! I must be having an out-of-body experience! This can't be Braswell actually saying nice things about me!

"He can do the job," Brazz went on, "and has demonstrated to me that he can do the job. Except for this present incident, I believe he has value to the service, and I would be willing to serve with him. I can't say with certainty how his integrity has developed since his first semester last year, but if he can learn from this and perhaps complete some sort of remediation course, I think he would be commissionable."

Brazz paused, glanced down a second, then back at the board. "Mister Gantar did come to me about a week and a half ago and told me he was guilty and that he had decided it was best to tell everything he knew and get it off his chest. He told me he had been having some problems that he was trying to work out through counseling, and that he wanted to apologize to me for not living up to my trust. I . . . I think that's all I have to say, Sir."

"What is your opinion of his potential as a naval officer?" one of them asked.

"I think he does have potential as a naval officer, yes, Sir," Brazz answered, without hesitation. "He has worked with his troops, and he's shown some good concern for them. Over the past year, he's begun setting an excellent example for his troops."

"Any questions from the board?" Admiral Allen asked, to no response. "Any questions of your company officer, Mister Gantar?"

Are you kidding? And break the spell? "No, Sir," I managed.

Lieutenant Commander Braswell was excused, and I tried to get a grip on my amazement. Braswell! He had actually put in a good word—for him, an enthusiastic endorsement! At that moment, I thought I could have kissed him . . . almost. Good old Brazz; heck of a guy! Comes through in the pinch!

And then Admiral Allen was speaking again. "Midshipman Gantar, you now have the opportunity to present matters for consideration by this board. Do you have any documents that you would like to present?"

"Yes, Sir, I do." I picked up the packets I had prepared and made explanations as I passed them out. "Here's a copy of my performance last semester and my grades, and—you may already have this, Sir, but I included an affidavit of NIG's treatment of the midshipmen during their investigations."

"Yes, we've seen this before," the admiral snapped. "It will be attached to your record."

"Yes, Sir." The packets also contained records of the courses I took prior to EE311, biographical information, and a personal statement. The personal statement was the linchpin of my strategy, if I had one. It would also be the most difficult part of my hearing.

"Sir, if I might be granted a slight deviation from the normal procedure, I'd like to briefly introduce my next witness. His appearance here is a bit unusual—"

"One moment, please," Admiral Allen muttered, without looking up from my packet. The board members continued reading my material.

"Is your grandfather still living?" one of them asked, again without looking at me.

"Yes, Sir, he is." And if I'd let him, he'd be here now and you'd be choking on his resumé and wishing you could figure out a way to separate his grandson without his knowledge—but it can't go down that way, Jeff, and you know it ...

Admiral Allen finished looking through my packet, shuffled the papers together, stacked them and laid them to one side. "The documents you've offered will be entered into the record. Do you wish to call any witnesses?"

"Yes, Sir, I do. Before I call him, could I make a brief statement?"

"Yes, go ahead."

Now that the crucial moment was here, I felt the words evaporating from my mind before I could utter them. Come on, Jeff! Think! This is your only shot! Tell them!

"Sir, I came here for one reason only: to tell the whole truth and make amends for my lapses in judgment and ethics. Part of that process demands that I tell you the truth about ... about myself— about who I really am. The doctor that I'm about to call is Lieutenant Commander Patten, a counselor here at the Academy. I started seeing him last October because ..." I gulped, felt my cheeks burning with embarrassment "... because I was sexually abused as a child."

I hurried on to tell them I didn't want their pity, wasn't trying for the sympathy vote. I just wanted them to know how far I was willing to go to give them the entire story, lay out for them the tortuous path that had led me to the Double-E, and the painful journey of self-discovery that would ultimately deliver me from the influences that had made my moral failure possible.

I told them how Dad and Grandpa had been willing to testify on my behalf and mobilize their collective influence and resources to help me. And then I told them I resisted such aid because I wanted the decision to be made only on my merits as a person and a potential naval officer. I told them I would rather be separated than retained on false pretenses.

And then I called in Doctor Patten.

Doc gave them his name and rank and described his duties at the Yard. Then I asked him to describe the circumstances of our meeting and the reasons I initially sought counseling.

"Mister Gantar came to the Counseling Center to request help in dealing with psychologically-based situational impotence."

I flinched inwardly when I heard the last word thump out into the room. I kept my eyes pinioned to Doc's face. I didn't dare steal a glance toward the board members.

"He was extremely anxious in any situation which involved any kind of sexual closeness—"

Not exactly your typical lusty Young Warrior, Your Honor—

" . . . He was very fearful that others might discover his difficulty . . . he had very low self-esteem, and he had numerous questions about his own normalcy and masculinity . . ."

So, if you ever had any doubts about kicking this guy out on his butt, how do you feel now, knowing how screwed up he used to be?

"He was obsessed," Doc went on. "He was so worried about his problem and how he was perceived that he sacrificed himself—trying to become whatever others wanted him to be.

"Baseball was an important facet of Mister Gantar's life. In his eyes, success in baseball made him more acceptable to his father. He came here on a baseball scholarship, but finding a solution to this problem came to overshadow even baseball. He quit the team in order to focus more time and energy on dealing with it."

If any of this was impressing the board, they gave no sign.

After he related my spontaneous memory of the abuse, I asked Doctor Patten to assess my progress.

"In a single word—amazing. Mister Gantar was, from the beginning, unusually open and honest in talking about his problems, despite the fact that it was very difficult for him to do.

"I began to see specific changes in his behavior. He acquired the ability to perceive relationships between his anxieties and the childhood abuse and to apply his insights to overcoming them. He began to realize how feelings related to the abuse had compromised his ability to live up to the principles he had always believed in."

I asked Doc to describe more fully the changes he had seen in me. He said I had gone from being a ship without a rudder or sails to being a person of principle—in control of my own destiny. He felt I was no longer controlled by what others thought of me, but rather that I was taking total responsibility for my own life and decisions. He mentioned the improvement in my academic performance and my willing participation in a support group at the clinic.

"When Mister Gantar revealed to me his involvement in the Double-E affair, I asked him what he was going to do. His response was that he intended to tell the truth and accept whatever consequences resulted. I asked him what he thought those consequences might be, and he replied that he thought there was a good chance he might be separated, but, because of what he had learned about himself, it was more important to him to do what was right than to be graduated from the Naval Academy."

Striving to keep my expression properly neutral, I asked him, "Sir, do you have an opinion of my character?"

He turned to face me and his eyes never left my face as he said, "Yes, I do. I think that Midshipman Gantar has always had solid principles. Largely because of the sexual abuse in his childhood, he has failed to live up to them for much of the last seventeen years, but I believe that now he makes the choices about what he does, what he says, and how he behaves based on theses principles. I see him as a man with intelligence, compassion, initiative, integrity, and an unusual degree of moral courage.

"What I'm about to say, I've only said about two other people, one of whom is my own son. In my opinion, Midshipman Gantar is one of the finest young men I know.

"I think his potential as a naval officer is outstanding. He can become the kind of officer his subordinates will be glad to follow, his peers would do well to emulate, and his superiors will respect . . . I would be very proud and pleased to serve with him in the Navy."

I felt a tremendous rush of gratitude clogging my throat. I wanted to thank Doc, to try and express my appreciation for his affirmation—a totally unexpected, but desperately needed, endorsement of Jeff Gantar as a person. But instead of attempting to convey all the things I was feeling, I pulled my eyes away from Doc, looked at Admiral Allen and said, "Sir, I have no more questions."

"Questions from the board?" he asked. There were none, and Doctor Patten was dismissed. The admiral looked at me and said, "Do you wish to make a statement?"

I took a deep breath. One more hurdle to go. "Yes, Sir, I do."

"Go ahead."

I told them of my lifelong struggle for acceptance and approval, of my chronic low self-esteem. I talked about my perceptions of how the childhood incident of abuse had affected my perception of myself as a person. I reiterated that I wasn't trying to excuse any of my actions, just to understand them.

"When I was four years old, my dad was just back from Vietnam. They were going out and hired a babysitter to watch my nine-year-old brother and me. And while my brother was watching TV, she took me to an upstairs bathroom and locked the door and . . . and she molested me. I was four years old, and I didn't know what was going on, and it was really scary, and . . . I was only four, and I just didn't know how to deal with it, or why such a horrible thing should be happening to me.

"But, for some reason, I still knew it was wrong, terribly wrong. I just couldn't understand why, couldn't find the answers to my confusion and fear. And as a child, I blamed myself to a great degree. I turned it in on myself, and thought maybe I was bad, and had somehow caused it to happen. I was only four, and though with hindsight it's easy to see a little kid couldn't be at fault, when you're four years old, things aren't nearly so clear.

"And so, I began to believe I was a bad person, an unlovable, unacceptable person. I used to lie in bed and ask God, 'Why am I so bad? Why am I so rotten?' But I never got any answers . . . My parents still loved me, it seemed, and I began to think that as long as I made them proud, maybe I was okay, maybe I was acceptable. And so I began to do anything I could to win their approval."

I noticed Captain McGann sobbing softly into a crumpled handkerchief. Lieutenant Commander Tinker, my counsel, was sniffing and wiping her eyes. The board members were more wide-eyed and attentive now than they had been at any time during the hearing. I concentrated on maintaining my composure; Dad had told me it was important not to cry, not to appear weak. I felt a few drops running down my cheeks, but my voice stayed firm and clear.

This is what Grandpa Karl must have meant by counting on God no matter what way things are going to work out. What was happening around me, as far as the academy degree, as far as my career and what I think—that wasn't important. What was important was my relationships, my love, my standing with God. I never thought there was life after the academy, but there is, there always is with God.

I was drawing upon reserves of strength I never suspected I had. At last I was telling my story, and I had to get to the end.

"I would spend fifteen hours a day taking batting practice from a pitching machine in my backyard—trying to become a great ballplayer like my dad. Once in high school, I made All-State in baseball, batted over .400, and I felt absolutely great because I felt I had earned my parents' approval."

I talked about my fear of intimacy, about my shame in the realization that I was so different from my friends in my attitude toward girls, my terror of being discovered for the charlatan I knew myself to be. I told them about being accepted, about the exhilaration of getting into the Academy, the thrill of achieving something so precious to my father and grandfather. I talked about Plebe Summer, about being ranked first in my company during both sets.

"I thought the bad feelings would go away if I could have these kinds of accomplishment, but they didn't. I went through Plebe Year and into Youngster Year still dealing with inadequacy, fear of rejection, and feelings of inferiority. I began to notice that a lot of guys who seemed normal were heavy into the party scene. I decided that was an avenue I should examine. And so, I tried to overachieve in that area, just as I had striven to overachieve in every other area of my life. Even though, deep down, I knew it was wrong, I figured I had to fit in, to go along in order to be normal—whatever normal was.

"But it still didn't work. By second class year, I had become a skilled liar and hated myself for it. And then, I met a girl named Angie Miller; someone different from anyone I had ever met, and I knew I had to find some real answers to my problems if I wanted to develop any kind of normal relationship with her. During that time, the memory of the abuse resurfaced, and I told her about it, scared to death she would hate me for it—but she didn't. And the next Monday, I told Lieutenant Commander Patten, and he didn't reject me, either. And that was how the process of healing began, the process that has brought me here today."

They were all looking directly at me, their notes and other papers forgotten. I had to finish, to drive home whatever it was I wanted them to remember as they made their deliberations. I glanced at my notes, then tried to make eye contact with each of them in turn as I concluded.

"I've learned a great many lessons from all this. First of all, I've learned to rely on myself. I've learned that I don't have to satisfy other people's needs, and that I can't control what others think of me. I've learned that you can't solve problems by sidestepping them, or by lying to an honor board and getting retained because you didn't own up to the truth. And I've learned that I must stand on my own two feet. I'm finished with leaning on anyone else, even some-one I love as much as I love my father.

"The first time I got in honor trouble, as Lieutenant Comman-der Braswell mentioned earlier, my dad flew in a lawyer to go to bat for me in case I got kicked out. And I allowed him to do it. I am no longer willing to allow anyone to keep me from taking a rap I deserve in the manner in which I believe I must take it. This situa-tion has placed me at odds with my father—a circumstance which, a few months ago, would have been unthinkable to me. But, despite my continuing love and respect for my dad, I cannot allow anyone to assume responsibility or accountability for my actions and deci-sions other than myself.

"I've also learned about what it means to be a true friend—one who doesn't tell you whatever you want to hear, but who instead is willing to give the most precious gift of all—the truth. As I sit before you today, I realize that, despite the circumstances, I have a deep sense of satisfaction. I've decided on the correct course of action, and I've taken it, to the best of my ability. That sense of per-sonal integrity is something that can never be taken away from me, no matter what happens. That's all I have to say, Sir."

"Midshipman Gantar, do you have anything further to add?" Admiral Allen asked, after a pause.

"I think I've said everything, Sir."

"Very well. The board will now close to deliberate."

"Attention on deck!" called Lieutenant Secor, as the board members rose to leave the room. I stood and watched them file out. None of them looked at me as they left. The whole process had taken less than two hours. Two hours—and one entire lifetime.

I would find out my fate after all scheduled hearings had been conducted.

And now . . . We wait.

☆ 15 ☆
No-Man's Land

AFTER MY ALLEN BOARD, I felt an overwhelming sense
of release. At last, it was over! No matter what the board
decided, I had done everything I could possibly do to make things
right. Finally, the ball was well and truly in someone else's court.

Lieutenant Commander Tinker told me to wait in the lobby
until they had finished deliberating my case. In their closed conference, they would discuss all the facts presented at my hearing,
along with Dr. Patten's testimony and the things I had told them.
The expression on their faces at the end of my hearing was unlike
anything I had seen during the proceedings at which I had testified.
They seemed to be really listening to me, really trying to absorb and
understand what I was saying, not just going through a rote procedure so they could get to the next name on the list. I had the crazy
thought, close to the end, that Admiral Allen might actually get up
from his chair and come shake my hand.

He didn't, of course, nor did any of the others. But as Lieutenant Commander Tinker and I sat in the lobby longer and longer,

she began to look at her watch and mutter things like, "What's taking them so long? I've never seen them deliberate this long before ..." Evidently, a typical post-hearing conference was ten minutes or so, tops. The eternal optimist in me began to whisper that they might be preparing to do the unthinkable: retain me, despite my confession!

After a forty-five-minute conference, they finally came out of the room. My heart in my throat, I stared at them as they walked back into the boardroom for the next hearing, hoping for some clue, some hint of what they had decided about me. I don't know what I expected—a smile maybe, or just a slight nod from one of them. Heck, why not a big thumbs-up and a couple of high fives?

But they never looked at me, never acknowledged my presence as they filed back into the hearing room. It was as if they didn't want to see me or be reminded of anything about me. At that moment, I had the unwelcome, unsurprising sense that I was done for, as far as the Navy was concerned. But there was no way to know for sure until their decision was actually announced, probably sometime in April. Until then I, like everyone else who had gone into the boardroom and sat in the chair of the accused, would have to live on a mixture of hope and fear.

☆   ☆   ☆

IT WAS NOW LATE March, the point in the semester when the second class starts getting hyped about the Ring Dance, when they receive their Academy class rings. And, of course, the firsties were getting Gold Stripe Fever. Graduation was just around the corner, and the top of Jacob's Ladder was within arm's reach.

For some. For those of us who were waiting for the Allen Board to announce our fates, these days were sheer torture. We were watching those who had managed to remain untainted by Double-E don the broad, confident grins of righteous acolytes about to be assumed into the Holy of Holies. Meanwhile, the 115 of us who had been to Allen Boards felt like Rush Limbaugh at a Democratic fundraiser—only worse. We were islands of despair in a surging sea of hilarity.

Some of us, however, were bigger lepers than others. Those of us who had told the truth at our boards found ourselves despised by the majority of accused who had been less forthcoming in their testimony. One day, I went out to my car—an '87 maroon Acura Integra—and found several long, deep gashes which ran from headlights to rear bumper. Somebody had keyed my car. I don't know who did it, but amid all the isolation and ostracism I was receiving from nearly every quarter, this gutless act of vandalism was almost too much to handle. My peers hated me, my family doubted me, and Angie was showing the strain of hanging in.

Not only that, but the euphoria that had enveloped me after my Allen Board was long gone. I had a serious case of buyer's remorse. Had I done the honorable thing, or had I committed the greatest blunder of my entire life? I had to admit that at this point, the signs weren't encouraging.

On 31 March, I was summoned to the commandant's conference room in Bancroft Hall to hear the decision of the Allen Board. Dressed in flawless service dress blues, I waited in a long line of anxious first-class midshipmen. The atmosphere was tense—so tense that we must have looked like black dominoes set in a row. And no one wanted to fall.

Waiting in silence, I wondered about the words I would hear in a few minutes. Would they give life to my dream or force me to venture out into the wilderness? For four years, the Navy had been all I knew—or wanted to know. What would happen if I fell off the ladder? Where would I land?

A mid burst out of the conference room, hugged his family, and high-fived a couple of his friends. Maybe there was hope! The Board seemed to be retaining most of the mids. There was Duke and the football players—all smiles. The line was moving fast—whatever the words were, they didn't take long. Then it was my turn.

I walked into the boardroom and stood at parade rest at the foot of the table as Admiral Allen read a copy of the report he would file with the chief of naval operations.

"On 22 March 1994, the Honor Review Board conducted a hearing in the case of Midshipman First Class Gantar. . . . Midshipman Gantar was charged with cheating and lying.

"At the hearing, Midshipman Gantar pled guilty to the charges. In accordance with this plea, the board found that Midshipman Gantar had violated the honor concept. . . . The board also considered evidence of Midshipman Gantar's potential to develop the proper sense of personal honor required of a commissioned officer."

And then, the phrase that froze my blood.

"The board then determined that Midshipman Gantar should be recommended for separation from the Naval Academy. In accordance with the precept, the board reviewed and affirmed this disposition after all cases had been heard."

I don't know how I kept from fainting, but somehow I remained upright. Admiral Allen started to put the report aside and dismiss me, but Captain Sutton nudged his elbow and whispered something to him, pointing at a paragraph on the report. The admiral glanced at Sutton, then at me, cleared his throat, and read the indicated passage.

"The board notes favorably that Midshipman Gantar pled guilty to serious misconduct. Since his involvement in the compromise, Midshipman Gantar has actively sought to correct his mistakes, including actively seeking and being selected as company honor representative. The clarity and sincerity of his testimony and cooperation were without equal."

Admiral Allen glanced again at Captain Sutton then put the report aside for the last time.

So, that's it. I'm separated. I'm out. Off the ladder. It really happened . . .

"Midshipman Gantar, do you have any questions about the disposition of your case?" Admiral Allen was asking.

Somehow I was able to raise my eyes to his face and answer in a firm voice, "No, Sir."

"Very well. You are dismissed."

I came to attention and wheeled toward the door. As I walked out, LCDR Braswell said, "Gantar, you . . . you're going to be okay. You're going to make it." I was a little surprised, and I wasn't sure what he meant, but I knew that he was right.

"Yes, Sir, I will." We nodded at each other, and I walked out of the building.

Dazed, I made my way to my room, threading through the scores of celebrating midshipmen. I fell onto my rack and wondered about Brian. He had good grades, good performance—maybe he would be safe. Then he walked into the room, and the look on his face dashed my last hope. He was separated.

☆   ☆   ☆

WHEN I RECEIVED MY copy of the report, I noted that the board had recommended to CNO that I not be required to repay the cost of my education at the Academy, which came to about $58,000. Well, that's something, at least. Not much, when compared to a life just tossed on the dungheap, but something . . .

The first person I called was Angie. I told her I had to see her as soon as possible, but I didn't tell her why. When she picked me up at about 1630 that afternoon, I told her I'd been separated. At first, she was incredulous. Then silent tears began to pour uncontrollably down her cheeks. As reality began to sink in, fear and confusion fought for control of her thoughts. She couldn't look at me, couldn't talk to me; she just held her face in her hands and wept. And who could blame her? All our plans for the future hinged upon my graduation and commissioning. Now everything was up for grabs. At that moment, I wished I'd lied to the Allen Board.

Angie told me later that she needed to pray for guidance. Ultimately she believed that God had a bigger plan than we did. We just didn't know it at the time.

That night, I called my dad. Somewhat to my surprise, he didn't react in anger to the news; it was more like resigned exhaustion. He hadn't had a decent night's sleep since I first revealed the Double-E situation to him back at Christmas. "Jeff, son, I knew this would happen," he said in a flat voice. "They don't care about you, they don't care about doing the honorable thing. I wish you'd listened to me."

Jon, Terry, and all the other guys who had lied and covered up in their Allen Board hearings were retained. They were jubilant, openly celebrating their successful skate past the final barriers to their graduations. Needless to say, they had little sympathy for people like Brian and me, whom they viewed as having obstructed their attempts to survive and graduate. "Gantar, man, all you had to do was keep quiet! No one confesses after they lie initially—it's suicide! Too bad, but that's the way this place works . . ."

There were many, many moments when I felt like a world-class fool. I had told the truth—even convinced others to do so!—and was being expelled, while those who had lied till they died would be commissioned as ensigns in the United States Navy. I just couldn't get my mind around the gross injustice of the situation.

For Grandpa, the injustice was the worst. As much as anything, he felt betrayed by the service to which he had given the best years of his life. He was a devoted Navy man, and he just couldn't believe the Navy would deal so harshly with me while letting known liars go scot-free. Even beyond the personal pain of watching his grandson suffer, the pain of disappointment in the organization weighed heavily on him.

In many ways, Doctor Patten helped me survive those days. He was always available, always willing to talk. He helped me keep things in perspective, helped me remember that there were greater issues involved than a career in the Navy or my personal plans or

even the dark pit of disappointment that my family and I were grop-
ing through. I really had the sense that he knew, in some way, what
I was feeling. It was as if he had been brought into my life for that
very time, when I desperately needed the friendship of someone like
him. I don't think our relationship was an accident.

The truth of Grandpa Karl's letter came back to me once again.
Though I had run from God and despaired of ever being able to
approach him, I now realized that he had never given up on me, and
had, in fact, drawn near to me. He had heard even the prayers of
desperation I had uttered from a hopeless heart. He had placed
people in my life who could help me learn to tolerate the light, even
to embrace it.

And the other amazing thing is that, despite everything—the
humiliation, the anger, the anxiety over the future, and all the rest
of it—I could find within myself a calm center of reassurance. To
my amazement, I began to realize that I would survive this travesty.
The old Jeff Gantar would have been obliterated by it, but I
wouldn't be. Not only did truth heal; it also strengthened. I began
to verify in my own life the eternal wisdom of the words, "The truth
shall set you free."

And what can I say about Angie? That she was a blessing from
God? I drew closer to God by learning to love her and learning
about the love between us. And I love God more for giving me such
an incredible and wonderful person. I will argue, though many
would argue the same thing for their partners, that she is the most
wonderful girl in the whole world.

When the Allen Board decisions were announced, in late March
and early April, the news media descended on Annapolis like buz-
zards on a dead horse. CNN, ABC, CBS, NBC, USA Today, Esquire,
Forbes, the *Washington Post*—everybody was there having a grand
old time. Many of the mids who had gone to Allen Boards were only
too happy to loudly declare their misfortunes to anyone who would
listen—preferably, anyone with a microphone or minicam.

I wanted no part of the media circus. I wasn't interested in justifying myself to anyone. I had said what I needed to say to the only group that needed to hear: the Allen Board. Many of the guys who were guilty as sin were grabbing anyone who looked like a reporter and spouting reams of their whitewashed versions of events. The whole thing made me sick.

Even Brian got sucked in, to a degree. He was talking to some people with the *Capital* and some other newspapers and urging me to get involved in telling my side of the story. "If we don't speak up, no one will ever know what really happened. All those other guys are out there, dumping their load of crap on America. Why shouldn't we get a chance to be heard?"

I knew he had a point, but it just didn't feel right to me. For one thing, I was still hoping against hope I could stay in the Navy. My case was still pending with the chief of naval operations. I wasn't sure of the wisdom of spouting a bunch of anti-Yard vitriol while making any attempt at all to remain in the Navy's good graces.

Crazy though it may sound, something deep within me still believed in the United States Navy. Despite the hazing, the hypocrisy, and all the other gross imperfections of the Academy, I still wanted to serve my country in a Navy uniform, as my grandfather had. I just wasn't interested in trashing the Navy so some reporter could get a juicy story for the evening edition.

In addition, my dad and grandfather had advised against such self-serving strategies as vilifying the Navy in the press. "You're guilty, you confessed, and you're already separated," they said. "At least leave with some dignity, some class." That sounded correct to me.

I made an exception to my no-press policy in the case of Frank Cerabino, a reporter for the *Palm Beach Post*. For starters, Cerabino was a 1977 graduate of the Academy, so I knew he understood the background and probably wasn't too interested in sensationalizing the story. Also, he had been in contact with my family before calling me, and I didn't think my dad or grandfather would have given the time of day to some rumormongering scoopmeister. So, I told him what had happened, from the night before the Double-E all the way through my Allen Board decision.

One day Brian and I went to see our attorneys about the progress of our appeals. When we arrived, we knew immediately that the press was there; a group of ten or twelve mids was bunched around a professional-looking woman who was asking the usual questions: "Tell me what happened . . . Do you think it was fair? . . . How were you interrogated? . . . Were you guilty? . . ." I saw some of the guys who were retained despite their guilt, and they were telling the reporter things that made me want to vomit. They were like little birds in a nest, fighting each other to be the first to answer her questions, each trying to outdo the last with stories of cruel interrogations, unjust accusations, and wronged honor. It was a real free-for-all. Even the reporter seemed skeptical of some of the swill the mids were tossing her way.

After a while, the crowd lost interest and kind of drifted away. The reporter saw me sitting to one side, and came over. "Do you have something you'd like to tell about the Double-E?" she asked.

"No, ma'am, I don't feel like talking."

"Why not?"

I shifted uncomfortably in my chair. "Well, I don't really have anything controversial to say."

She gave me an appraising look, then asked, "Were you involved in the cheating?"

Looking past her, I replied, "Yes, ma'am."

I think my admission surprised her. "What happened? Are you separated?"

"I was separated, yes." I began to wish I hadn't allowed this conversation to begin.

"Tell me what happened," she pressed.

"Look, it's a long story, and—I just don't want to talk about it right now."

She looked at me for a while without saying anything, sensing my discomfort. "Could we maybe talk another time?" she asked, finally.

I shrugged. "Maybe. I don't know." She requested my name, and for some reason, I gave it. By then, more guys were coming in to continue the public crucifixion of the truth, and I left.

About a week later, she called. It turned out that she was an assistant producer with *60 Minutes*, and she wanted her producer to talk to me. They were at the Loew's Annapolis, she said, and were interviewing mids for possible inclusion in a story about the cheating scandal. Would I be willing to come down and talk?

Brian immediately went to work on me. "Come on, Jeff! You don't have to say anything you don't want to say. Just tell them your version: what you saw, what you heard, what you said . . . It's our chance, man! Let's do it!"

We went downtown to the hotel and talked with the *60 Minutes* people. Not surprisingly, Brian dominated the Q & A. At that point, I was content to sit back and allow him to do most of the talking. I still wasn't sure I really wanted to be there. They had told us the show wouldn't air until August, which would be way too late to have any impact on our situations with the Navy. What was the point?

After a while, the producer thanked Brian for coming down, but asked me to stay behind. Brian looked kind of puzzled, but he left.

The producer must have sensed I had something to add to the interview, but that for some reason, I was reluctant to talk. She told me how many mids they had interviewed and how disappointed they were with most of them. She felt there were huge gaps in most of their stories and sensed they were giving *60 Minutes* only what would make them look better. She emphasized how important it was to the show to get at the truth.

I began to feel more comfortable. If these people really wanted to know the truth, I could handle that. As long as they weren't primarily interested in smearing the Navy or the Academy or the mids involved, I thought I might have something valuable to say. So what if the show wouldn't air until August? That didn't matter anyway, since the only exoneration I was interested in would have to come from SecNav. I decided to give them my story—all of it.

When I finished, about thirty minutes later, the producer and her assistant were very quiet; the assistant was in tears. "Thank you, Jeff," the producer said. "You've given us the kind of thing we're after."

Of the scores of mids interviewed, *60 Minutes* chose perhaps a half-dozen to actually tape for the show: Brian, Dave Basset, Justin Jones-Lansky, me, and a couple of other guys whose interviews wound up on the cutting-room floor.

We wore our SDBs—Service Dress Blues—to the taping session. On the way to the hotel, Brian asked me if I'd thought about what I was going to say. At that moment, I was more worried about controlling the Alfalfa-style cowlick on the back of my head. I remember thinking, "Yeah, I know what I'm going to say. I'm just going to tell them the truth." I wondered if, once again, I was underestimating how intimidating the situation would be.

The entrance to the Loew's Annapolis looks like a set on "Lifestyles of the Rich and Famous." They weren't ready to begin taping when we got there, so they hustled us into a sort of makeshift Green Room for about ten minutes. As we sat there, I could tell the others were all getting pretty nervous. I started to feel a little guilty. Why am I not scared about this? Am I missing something here?

We went into the presidential suite, where everything was set up. We sat in chairs in front of lights as bright as the sun, and Morley Safer sat in front of us. The cameras rolled.

I remember that when Mr. Safer asked the first question, Brian just kind of looked at me, as if to say, "You're on." For the first time ever, he seemed to be clamming up.

When it was over, guys from the crew started coming up to me, shaking my hand, even asking for my autograph! It was weird. The producer told me I came across just as sincerely as when we'd been talking without the camera. I was glad, but I wondered how the tape would be edited. My dad had expressed misgivings about my talking to "60 Minutes." He was afraid they'd just make me look worse than I already did. It all depended on what they decided to use and how they put it together.

These doubts began to crowd in closer as we arrived back at the Academy. Had I done the wise thing? Would talking to the media hurt my chances with the CNO and SecNav? Perhaps naively, I was still praying that a miracle would happen, and that I would be retained.

And then, on 20 April, I got another little surprise from the Navy. The chief of naval operations—Admiral Kelso, the officer who was raked over the coals in the Tailhook investigation— upheld my separation and overruled the recommendation of the Allen Board with regard to repayment of my education bill. I now owed the U. S. government nearly $60,000. Great. I can't graduate, so I don't guess I'll be going into the Navy. I wonder how long it'll take me to pay back sixty grand on a payroll deduction, making $4.50 an hour at McDonald's? I appealed the CNO's decision to the secretary of the Navy. I was told I could expect his announcement within ten days.

My dad and Grandpa began calling their congressmen, writing letters, doing anything they could think of to win redress for me. At this point, I guess I felt helpless to stop them. $60,000! It might as well have been sixty million. There was no way I could ever pay it back. Being separated was bad enough, but this, too?

In the meantime, I decided to finish my coursework for the semester. Preparations for graduation were now in full swing, which made things much worse for guys like me. But I kept on going to classes, doing homework, writing papers, taking tests . . . What else could I do? At some point, after all appeals were exhausted and all results were in, I would have to pick up my life and go forward with it. I just kept putting one foot in front of the other and taking things a day at a time.

On 28 April, the SecNav's decision came down: I was separated, but I would not be required to repay the cost of my education. Additionally, all the separated midshipmen were on restriction to Academy grounds until the close of the academic term—in other words, until our last finals were taken. If we left the premises, we would be court-martialed.

My family became more depressed than ever. But, as I called home during the two weeks or so between SecNav's edict and the end of the semester, I could at times hear tendrils of acceptance, even forgiveness, in Dad's voice. I suppose, having reached the absolute bottom, he was beginning to have no choice but to start looking up, ever so cautiously.

Angie assured me repeatedly that she still loved me and would stick by me, but I knew she had never really considered the possibility of my actual dismissal from the Yard. Almost daily, she was seeing stories in the Baltimore newspapers and on T.V. about the cheating incident, about those who had been expelled. Meanwhile, since I was on restriction, Angie and I couldn't see each other. I knew I was pushing her love to the absolute limit, and I hated myself for it.

During the two weeks we were apart, we talked on the phone as much as we could. But it still wasn't like being able to hold and hug each other, and I missed her terribly. If I hadn't had God with me, and Dr. Patten, I would have been completely alone. Angie said she was just like a walking zombie. She was really depressed and needed me at that point just like I needed her. I was constantly praying, "I know you did this for a reason, God. Just show me why, just show me why."

I began to apply for admission to other universities in the area, so I could at least finish my engineering degree and stay close to Angie. But, of course, I was untouchable, having been expelled under serious conduct charges. Even Brian, with a 3.5 GPA, was getting turned down by school after school. All the separatees were stripped of our rank at the Academy and had to wear special insignia identifying us as "the cheaters." Naturally, the profs weren't about to cut us any slack in our coursework, but I was determined to finish the semester. Still, it was as close to leprosy as I ever want to come. Some of the guys quit going to class and left as soon as they were able. Chris Rounds, for example, was failing miserably and vanished from the Yard as soon as he could.

There's a saying in the Brigade: "That which doesn't kill me can only make me stronger." So far, I wasn't dead. I had discovered that I was capable of doing things others found impossible. I had found within myself the capacity for great moral courage. But the most difficult test still lay ahead: Graduation Day. I wouldn't be there, though. In fact, I left the Academy grounds for the last time after my courses were completed. The date was 12 May 1994 . . . my twenty-second birthday.

☆ 16 ☆

THE
BEGINNING

THE CREDITS START TO roll; *60 Minutes* is over. A voice-over announces the headlines of the local Seattle station's upcoming news broadcast, later that evening. I thumb the remote and the screen goes blank with a fading electronic crackle. I stare at the empty screen, my mind whirling through the events, the images, the sounds. Sorting, wondering, searching . . .

I feel Angie squeeze my hand. "Jeff, I'm so proud of you."

"Thanks. But I'm a little disappointed. They left out most of what I said—"

"Not that," she interrupted, nodding toward the TV. "You had no control over what they used and what they didn't. The only thing you could control was what you said, how you responded. And not just to *60 Minutes*. To—everything."

I looked at her, loving her, waiting to hear what else she would say.

"That's why I'm here," she continued. "That's why I want to be with you from now on. Because of that strength. There are more ways to risk your life than in physical danger," she said, looking deep into my eyes. "And you are one of the bravest people I've ever known. That's the bottom line."

I pulled her close to me. How could I ever be thankful enough for her love, her loyalty?

And other healings were taking place. A few days earlier, I had been over at my parents' home in Spokane. It had been a good visit and things had almost seemed like old times—only without the dark shadows in my mind. As I had gone toward the car to leave, Dad called me. He was standing on the front steps. "Yeah, Dad?" I said as I walked back toward him.

He met me halfway between the door and my car, and he gripped my shoulder and looked at me. "Son," he said, "this Academy thing has been the worst experience of my life—worse than anything in 'Nam. It slivered my insides to watch you suffer, and the torture was worsened by my frustration at your unwillingness to try everything possible to stay in the Academy.

"But, son," he said, tightening his grip on my shoulder, "everyone has to make his own path. Maybe," he continued, looking past me now, "that's why I had to go into the Army, into the Rangers. I had to do it for myself. And that's what you've done," he said, looking back at me. "You've become a real man, Jeff. Sixty thousand dollars of the government's money couldn't do it for you. You had to do it on your own."

We embraced, and again I felt as I had that night seven months ago, in the hot tub. *My father loves me. He approves of me.* And I found out God loves me. Things happen for a reason. God won't give you only good your whole life. There are going to be tests, there are going to be times when you are saying, "Why, God, why?" But he's given those times to you for a reason, and you just have to trust.

Thank you, God! Thank you, thank you, thank you . . .

I got up from the couch to get a glass of water. Pulling open the refrigerator door, I saw the notice, affixed with a magnet, of my acceptance at the University of Washington. Initially they had refused my application, but on appeal they reconsidered and let me in. I was starting classes in about three weeks. Small rays of light were beginning to peek through.

Drinking my water, I remembered something Morley Safer said to me after the session was over. He came up to me and shook my hand, thanking me for coming down to be interviewed. And then he looked into my eyes and said, in that famous, slightly gruff baritone voice, "You know, young man, you should be teaching ethics at the Naval Academy!"

Maybe so. But now I knew that wasn't really the point. It wasn't a matter of getting the Academy to admit wrongdoing or change their policies. It was a matter of healing for me, a matter of taking responsibility for my own life.

It was, pure and simple, a question of honor.

EPILOGUE

O N T H E E V E N I N G O F March 25, 1995, in the city of York, Pennsylvania, Jeff Gantar was married to Angie. It wasn't a military wedding, but the descriptions of it made me wish I had been there. Dr. Tom Patten had gone, and told me later that Jeff and Angie were the perfect bride and groom.

It was during the reception that Jeff's grandfather turned to Tom and said, "You know, I wish someone would tell the story about this whole Annapolis affair." Tom, now smiling, just nodded his head in agreement but left the announcement of our forthcoming book up to Jeff's discretion and timing.

Marrying Angie was only part of putting the past to rest—albeit a very significant part. After several attempts, Jeff was finally admitted to the University of Washington where he was graduated with a degree in engineering. He now resides with his bride in Portland, Oregon, and works for Precision Castparts Corp. as an engineer in their Management Development program.

And Dr. Patten? Well, he too, has moved on to "bigger and better things," as we say. After retiring from the Navy, Tom was appointed to the faculty of Abilene Christian University. He is an associate professor of psychology and already has won the respect and admiration of both faculty and students. He and Jeff continue their friendship via phone calls, e-mail, and a couple of visits each year.

On one such occasion, this past January, I was invited to dine with Tom, his wife, Karen, and their son, Todd. Jeff and Angie were there, too—all the way from Portland! It was great to be with each other again, reflecting on what had brought us all together in the first place. And the expressions of joy on the faces of Jeff, Angie, and Tom made my trek from Philadelphia to Abilene, Texas, well worth the trip.

I want to end by saying that many times during the course of writing this book, I weighed myself in Jeff's balance and was found wanting. Our nation desperately needs people like Jeff Gantar— people who are willing to take personal responsibility for their actions, who give themselves to pursue the highest standards of personal honor despite the consequences, and who are absolutely unwilling to sacrifice truth—even painful, inconvenient truth— for expediency or personal comfort. "You shall know the truth," says Jesus, "and the truth will make you free." Today, Jeff Gantar is a free man.

Michael O'Donnell
Philadelphia, Pennsylvania